Tropical Forest Archaeology in Western Pichincha, Ecuador

Ronald D. Lippi

University of Wisconsin—Marathon County

 Case Studies in Archaeology: Jeffrey Quilter, Series Editor

THOMSON

WADSWORTH

Australia • Canada • Mexico • Singapore • Spain
United Kingdom • United States

Anthropology Editor: *Lin Marshall*
Assistant Editor: *Analie Barnett*
Editorial Assistant: *Amanda Santana*
Marketing Manager: *Diane Wenckebach*
Project Manager, Editorial Production:
  Catherine Morris
Print/Media Buyer: *Rebecca Cross*
Permissions Editor: *Sarah Harkrader*

Production Service: *Mary E. Deeg,*
  Buuji, Inc.
Copy Editor: *Linda Ireland, Buuji, Inc.*
Cover Designer: *Rob Hugel*
Cover Image: *Ronald D. Lippi*
Text and Cover Printer: *Webcom*
Compositor: *Buuji, Inc.*

The logo for the Archaeology series is based on ancient Middle Eastern and Phoenician symbols for house.

Printed in Canada
1 2 3 4 5 6 7 06 05 04 03 02

For more information about our products,
contact us at:
Thomson Learning Academic Resource Center
1-800-423-0563

For permission to use material from this text,
contact us by:
Phone: 1-800-730-2214   **Fax:** 1-800-730-2215
Web: http://www.thomsonrights.com

Library of Congress Control Number: 2002113254

ISBN 0-534-61294-6

Wadsworth/Thomson Learning
10 Davis Drive
Belmont, CA 94002-3098
USA

Asia
Thomson Learning
5 Shenton Way #01-01
UIC Building
Singapore 068808

Australia/New Zealand
Thomson Learning
102 Dodds Street
Southbank, Victoria 3006
Australia

Canada
Nelson
1120 Birchmount Road
Toronto, Ontario M1K 5G4
Canada

Europe/Middle East/Africa
Thomson Learning
High Holborn House
50/51 Bedford Row
London WC1R 4LR
United Kingdom

Latin America
Thomson Learning
Seneca, 53
Colonia Polanco
11560 Mexico D.F.
Mexico

Spain/Portugal
Paraninfo
Calle/Magallanes, 25
28015 Madrid, Spain

www.wadsworth.com

wadsworth.com is the World Wide Web site for Wadsworth and is your direct source to dozens of online resources.

At *wadsworth.com* you can find out about supplements, demonstration software, and student resources. You can also send email to many of our authors and preview new publications and exciting new technologies.

wadsworth.com
Changing the way the world learns®

For Elba, Julia, and David

Contents

Figures and Tables

FIGURES

TABLES

Foreword

ABOUT THE SERIES

These case studies in archaeology are designed to bring students, in beginning and intermediate courses in archaeology, anthropology, history, and related disciplines, insights into the theory, practice, and results of archaeological investigations. They are written by scholars who have had direct experience in archaeological research, whether in the field, laboratory, or library. The authors are also teachers, and in writing their books they have kept the students who will read them foremost in their minds. These books are intended to present a wide range of archaeological topics as case studies in a form and manner that will be more accessible than writings found in articles or books intended for professional audiences, yet at the same time preserve and present the significance of archaeological investigations for all.

ABOUT THE AUTHOR

Ronald Lippi was born in 1949 in the prairie town of Luverne, Minnesota. Despite an early interest in things scientific, he certainly was not one of those kids who dreamed of becoming an archaeologist. In fact, in the 1960s he was much more interested in becoming an astronaut and decided to study aerospace engineering. Although he completed his engineering degree, what really excited him as an undergraduate at the University of Minnesota were the few anthropology courses he took as general studies electives. With that awakened interest, the career recipe was as follows: Measure two cups of travel in South America, mix in a heaping spoonful of intellectual curiosity and another of a taste for adventure, blend in a bowlful of hard work, add a twist of romanticism and a pinch of survivalism, bake at moderately high heat in graduate school at the University of Wisconsin, Madison, for several years and—voilà—a South American archaeologist armed with a Ph.D.

Lippi has spent a total of about eight years off and on since 1969 living and working in South America, most of that while practicing archaeology. He has some archaeological experience in Wisconsin and Illinois but has dedicated most of his career to a few projects in Ecuador, including the long-term exploration of western Pichincha province, the topic of this book. Lippi has lived during the last dozen or so years in the city of Wausau where he is professor of anthropology at the Marathon County campus of the University of Wisconsin Colleges, which is the freshman-sophomore transfer institution within the University of Wisconsin System. He also serves as chair of the 13-campus Department of Anthropology and Sociology that is spread around the state. With heavy teaching and administrative responsibilities, research necessarily takes a backseat, but hc has managed to keep forging ahead with the Western Pichincha Project for many years and says, "I expect to continue until the bite of a poisonous snake sends me to that great test pit in the sky." Despite the disappointment of having little time to conduct fieldwork, Lippi loves the classroom and hopes that this book will demonstrate his commitment to undergraduate teaching.

Ronald Lippi has presented many papers at professional conferences and published numerous articles on his projects in South America. This is his third book on Ecuadorian archaeology; he wrote the previous two in Spanish, and they were published in Ecuador. The first of those is titled (when translated to English) *The First Ecuadorian Revolution: The Development of an Agricultural Lifeway in Ancient Ecuador* (1996), and the second is the longer, more technical, Spanish version of the present book, *An Archaeological Exploration of Western Pichincha, Ecuador* (1998). Lippi has worked throughout his career in close association with Ecuadorian colleagues and students, a kind of collaboration he believes is essential. Speaking of collaboration with Ecuadorians, he is married to a woman from Quito, Elba Guerrón, and they have two children, one currently a university student and the other in high school.

ABOUT THIS CASE STUDY

The general public in North America is well aware of the importance of tropical forests. Even schoolchildren can recite the names of endangered animals and plants, and "Save the Rainforest" is a popular cry on college campuses. *Jungle* is a word that is not used much anymore, due to its negative connotations of a "green hell." We see the tropical forest as our friend, promising cures for disease and oxygen for the atmosphere, and it must be saved from destruction. But despite the popular attention given to the billions of acres of tropical forests that still remain on the globe, the general public knows very little about its native inhabitants and even less about their histories.

This book by Ronald Lippi is a valuable contribution to the Case Studies in Archaeology series for many reasons. He combines a discussion of the travails of conducting archaeology in the tropical forest with a discussion of the results of his research. Along the way, we learn of the natural setting of the forest zone and the special methods and techniques (e.g., soil coring and phosphate testing) used for doing archaeology in it. Of particular interest to the archaeologist are the strategies Lippi employed for site survey. Many North American archaeologists are accustomed to walking plowed fields after recent rains, during which boots may be muddied but artifacts may be fairly easily found. Like many archaeologists working in densely wooded regions, the tropical forest archaeologist has to be innovative in developing ways to find sites, basically using every opportunity to examine bare ground and to obtain local knowledge.

In addition to exploiting every possible means to identify archaeological sites, Ronald Lippi reached back to the early historical records of the region. The use of records written by the Spanish Conquistadors about what they saw and about what the Incas told them of their own explorations and conquests is an important resource for Andean archaeology. Lippi clearly used this to his great advantage in his own research. Equally important, he took advantage of the local knowledge of the present-day native inhabitants of the region, particularly members of the Tsáchila nation. This kind of cooperative research is becoming increasingly more common in Latin America and elsewhere. It promises much for the future because it integrates the interests of the two groups that have the greatest personal stake in understanding the ancient past, the local descendents of prehistoric peoples and archaeologists.

We really do need to know as much as we can about the tropical forest. The best people to teach modern urban-dwellers about these places are the people who live in them and have lived in them for thousands of years. How and why people exploited the natural environment and the mistakes that they made and the lessons they learned can be of great value to us whether or not we ever live in the tropical forest. In this book, Ronald Lippi tells of his own successes and mistakes in an engaging style that will pull the reader into his work and the place to which he has devoted much of his professional career. It is a pleasure and a privilege to include his story in the Case Studies in Archaeology series.

Jeffrey Quilter
Washington, D.C.

Preface

I frequently tell students in my classes that archaeology is mostly a matter of common sense, that it is not rocket science (though since I have a university degree in aerospace engineering, I suppose I am a "rocket scientist" of sorts). I try to emphasize that archaeology is a relatively young discipline and, for the most part, its analyses and interpretations are not heavily dependent on sophisticated mathematics, statistics, or complex theories, so that any reasonably alert student who cares to devote some time and energy to its study can understand what archaeologists are writing and talking about. At the same time, I warn them that some archaeologists seem to have carried confusion to a high art form by the use of stilted language, excessive jargon, and poor writing skills so that common sense is sometimes hidden by a flood of words.

Since I preach this to my students on a regular basis, I have unwittingly set myself up for scathing criticism when I write a book to be read by those very same students, not to mention my colleagues who do not really take a fancy to my gratuitous critiques. While writing this book, I accordingly made a conscious effort to use common sense to the utmost, only to find that it may not be as common as it ought to be, at least in my circumstances. I also have tried to write clearly and in an occasionally enjoyable way with the idea that most of the readers of this book will be bright people, but will have little previous knowledge or understanding of archaeological methods and techniques.

That explains my writing style. Now what about the content of this case study? While nearly everyone knows that archaeologists excavate, few people have any idea how archaeologists find the sites or, in common parlance, "know where to dig." The other kind of fieldwork, surveying, comprises a number of strategies and methods for locating archaeological sites. With so much emphasis in the case study literature on excavation, I wanted to present to students a detailed look at surveying, since its role in archaeology is arguably as important as that of digging. So this book is primarily about a multiyear surveying project, though two chapters deal with coring and preliminary excavations at one site and another deals with ethnohistory, which is the use of historical documents regarding the history and culture of nonliterate peoples.

One might expect that a useful case study on archaeological surveying would be about a fairly classic approach to surveying in a familiar environmental zone. Such is not the approach in this book. This is an improvised, experimental approach to surveying in a region that even today is largely tropical rainforest with very rugged mountains and other obstacles that make traditional methods mostly useless. This is the kind of region that many of my professional colleagues would never consider tackling. In fact, early in the project, a few of my colleagues responded more or less in this way: "You're going to survey where? Are you kidding?" Since I had already "staked out," as a graduate student, a region and time period on the Ecuadorian coast and was recognized as having some small amount of expertise, it seemed to some of them senseless to set off on some impractical project in the jungle. Being too dense, perhaps, to understand the futility of my proposal, I charged ahead, found myself in a seemingly impossible situation, and gradually worked out a strategy that proved to be very valuable. It was probably persistence even more than common sense that carried this project through, but I suspect that these improvisations will turn out useful to others in similarly challenging situations.

The native peoples who are the object of this study were known to the Spanish in the 1500s as the Yumbos and the Niguas; they have not really survived to contemporary times. They are almost unheard of even in Ecuador, where the study of prehistory is compulsory in schools throughout the country. In the process of devising an opportunistic surveying strategy, I was also able to uncover some valuable archaeological information to augment considerably our knowledge of these peoples who have more or less vanished from the modern world. The effects of the Inca conquest of northern Ecuador and of the Spanish conquest of the Incas just a few decades later are also understood a little more clearly from this study. A portion of Ecuador, the western part of Pichincha province, which was previously almost completely unknown, is now a chapter in Ecuadorian prehistory. As the project continues into the future and more excavations are carried out, this knowledge is likely to be expanded and greatly improved.

With this goal in mind—presenting, in an easy-to-read style, the results of a regional archaeological survey carried out in a challenging environment with reliance on practical methods—I invite the reader to "dig in" and learn more about archaeology.

ACKNOWLEDGMENTS

Research projects in modern times are not done alone but with the help of many people, and it is here that I acknowledge and express gratitude to the many individuals and institutions who made this project possible through funding, fieldwork, intellectual stimulation, and logistical support.

The Western Pichincha Project was funded for the first two and a half years entirely by the Archaeology Museum of the Central Bank of Ecuador in Quito. I am particularly indebted to the Ecuadorian government, Museum administrators (principally Hernán Crespo Toral), and my Ecuadorian archaeology colleagues who supported the project and provided valuable input. Once I left Ecuador and returned to the United States, the project was suspended for a few years and then moved forward sporadically over several succeeding years. During that time, financial support came from my current academic institution, the University of Wisconsin Colleges, and from my campus, the University of Wisconsin—Marathon County, through its local foundation. I also received support for the project as a Fulbright Scholar through the J. William Fulbright Scholarship Board and the United States Information Agency. Some additional modest funding in recent years came from the Maquipucuna Foundation, an environmental protection foundation in Ecuador that operates the Maquipucuna Cloud Forest Preserve in Western Pichincha as well as other projects in Ecuador. The obsidian source analysis described in Chapter 8 was funded by a National Science Foundation grant (SBR-9802366) to the Missouri University Research Reactor. An earlier, expanded version of four sections in Chapter 5 of this book was originally published in the *Journal of Field Archaeology,* a publication of Boston University. Finally, the longer, more technical, Spanish version of this book was published through funds provided by the Interamerican Development Bank to the Pichincha provincial government and the Pontifical Catholic University of Ecuador.

All of my work in Ecuador was made possible through permits issued by and the support of the National Institute of Cultural Heritage, an office of the Ecuadorian Ministry of Education and Culture. The Catholic University in Quito also supported my research indirectly by allowing me to supplement my income in Ecuador by teaching archaeology classes. Ernesto Salazar, former director of archaeology at the Central Bank of Ecuador in Quito and of the Jijón y Caamaño Museum at Catholic University, was instrumental in helping me secure support for the project and in editing the longer Spanish version of this book.

Many people from throughout Western Pichincha are also partly responsible for any success this project has had. Almost without exception, the hundreds of local inhabitants with whom we interacted were helpful, friendly, and hospitable. A few of them made outstanding contributions, among whom I will mention Oseas Espín and Adán Ortiz of Nanegal and Héctor Arias of Mindo. Among the archaeology students and other helpers who played big roles in the field or laboratory work are Marco Suárez, Oswel Bahamonde, Servio Córdova, and Fabián Villalba. Other significant collaborators in one way or another in this project have been Hernán Crespo Toral, Dr. Frank Salomon, Patricia Estévez, Dr. María del Carmen Molestina, Myriam Roldán, Santiago Ontaneda, Marcelo Villalba, Olaf Holm, Elba Guerrón (my wife), and Bob Lippi (my brother), who read the manuscript chapter by chapter and kept telling me I had to make it less boring. If I have failed in that regard, it is not his fault.

Thanks also go to my esteemed colleague Dr. Jeffrey Quilter, editor of the Archaeology Case Studies series, and to Lin Marshall and Analie Barnett, editor and assistant editor, respectively, of anthropology publications at Wadsworth. Despite the best efforts of these individuals and the many archaeologists who provided support, encouragement, and advice over the years, I bear full responsibility for any errors as well as for the two or three bits of dazzling insight carefully hidden in these pages.

1/A Visit to the Tsáchilas[1]

As Alfredo Santamaría and I drove along a narrow dirt road through the patches of jungle and open pastures just southwest of the city of Santo Domingo de los Colorados, Ecuador (Figure 1.1), we noticed a large wooden sign painted in bright colors advertising in Spanish: "Colorado curer / The only son and heir of the herbal science of Gerónimo Calazacón[2] / Always open." The name on the sign was that of a "governor" of the tribe, who now augmented his subsistence by performing shamanic rituals and preparing herbal remedies for people who came from all over the country for medical or other supernatural help from him or other tribal healers.

We parked our Jeep a short distance from the pink wooden house on stilts and began to approach on foot. A yelping dog, which served in place of a doorbell for the house, ran toward us in a mildly threatening manner. Near the base of the thatched-roof house, I called out a greeting in Spanish and could hear some movement inside one of the rooms. There were two enclosed rooms on the upper level, a bedroom on the left side and a kitchen on the right. Between them was a living room with a back wall and two side walls; the front was open to the elements except for a low wooden rail. A man who appeared to be in his forties came out of the bedroom and stood at the rail looking down to us at ground level. We explained who we were and he invited us up the steps to the living room.

This man was one of the civil leaders of the Tsáchila nation, known to most Ecuadorians as the "Colorado" tribe. In Spanish *colorado* means red, and the Spanish have always referred to them as the "red Indians" because of their dress and body decoration. Men customarily use a thick bright red paste in their hair, made from a native seed (*annatto*) that is used in the United States and elsewhere today as a natural food colorant. Men and women traditionally wore striped wrap-around skirts, and the men carried a bright yellow or red blanket or wrap hung over a shoulder (Figure 1.2). Both usually went about bare-chested until non-natives taught the women to be ashamed of showing their breasts. Our host had the red paste on his scalp and was bare-chested except for some horizontal blue body stripes, but he

---

[1]Pronounced roughly as SAH-chee-lahs.
[2]While Calazacón is a common Tsáchila surname, the specific name used here is a fictitious one, since I did not request permission to identify the individual.

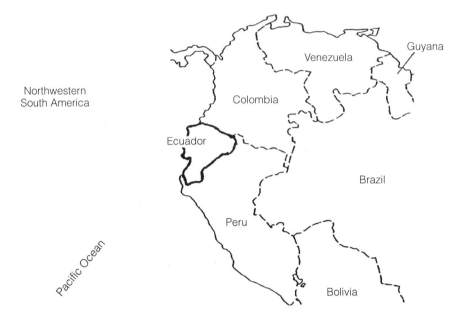

Figure 1.1 Maps showing location of Ecuador in northwestern South America and of the Western Pichincha research region within Ecuador

Chuck Lippi

Figure 1.2 Tsáchila family outside their home near Santo Domingo de los Colorados

wore, as do most Tsáchila men today, a pair of blue jeans in place of the traditional wrap-around garment.

We had sought him out for permission to interview various elders of the tribe regarding some petroglyphs (rock art) that we had found during our archaeological research. We hoped the elders might know something about the images or be able to interpret the symbols. It is necessary to get permission from leaders of the tribe because the Tsáchilas have been reeling for the past century under the unrelenting onslaught of outsiders who have taken away nearly all their land and disrupted their traditional culture. The Tsáchilas are understandably reticent to discuss their traditional practices with outsiders (except for their curing practices, from which some can now make a decent living) in light of the sustained effort by Christian missionaries and the Ecuadorian government to assimilate them.

No one knows how large the Tsáchila nation was before the Spanish came, and there is considerable uncertainty about the extent of their former territory. What we know, however, is that there are around a thousand Tsáchilas today and that they have been reduced to living on eight tiny "communes," or reservations, outside the bustling, fast-growing tropical city of Santo Domingo that now occupies a small part of their ancient homeland. The Tsáchilas are engaged in a peaceful struggle to stay alive as a nation and to retain their language and other essentials of their culture.

Another group known as the Chachis (or "Cayapas" to outsiders) some 200 km to the north is somewhat more numerous due to their greater isolation from the outside world even today, but they are engaged in a similar if less frantic struggle for existence. Finally, there is the tiny group calling itself the Awa-Kwaiker, who live near the Ecuadorian-Colombian border on the western slope of the Andes. The

Tsáchila, Chachi, and Awa-Kwaiker are three remnant nations that may be the only survivors of countless populous Indian nations that settled the lands of western Ecuador millennia ahead of the Spanish. They are apparently the last living links to the prehistoric past of the Western Pichincha region.

What happened to all the rest? The question is not merely one of historical curiosity. True, we want to know what became of these people, but our interest in archaeology does not stop there. We want to know to whom they are related, why they settled in the region, how they adapted to it, what their worldview was, how they interacted with neighboring peoples, what ideology influenced their values and beliefs; that is, we want to understand their lifeways—their culture—as well as their history.

And our interest goes even beyond that. In the modern world, recent settlers in the tropical rainforests have shown themselves conspicuously ignorant and even contemptuous of the rainforests and have proceeded to destroy these precious and fragile habitats with a vengeance. Isn't it possible that, despite our technological achievements and our arrogance, we could learn from the world's native tropical peoples how to live in that delicate environment without destroying it? Does it seem outlandish to suggest that peoples who survived in these forests for millennia have (or had, in the case of those who were killed off or assimilated) knowledge and understanding that could benefit contemporary peoples who do incalculable damage in a single generation? The question is not whether it is a good idea to acquire that knowledge, but whether that knowledge can even be recovered before it is lost forever. Despite frequent Hollywood hype about esoteric discoveries, treasure-hunting, and romanticism, archeology can be much more than a mere scholarly pursuit that satisfies our curiosity about the past; it can also provide valuable insight for resolving some of the great challenges of the modern world—challenges such as war, overpopulation, hunger, and environmental degradation, all of which seem to have their origins ultimately in antiquity.

We did not get very far with the Tsáchilas, through no fault of theirs or ours. A subsequent interview with one elder went all right, but we never got beyond that for a few years. Alfredo was my obligatory government contact with the tribe, and he was injured in a serious bus accident a short time later. As often happens in research, a potentially worthwhile avenue of discovery could not be pursued and would have to be attempted again when luck was on our side. The archaeology project described in this book is ongoing; there is much more we would like to do (including the Tsáchila interviews), but this book describes the substantial amount that has already been accomplished.

The following chapters summarize what we learned, how we learned it, and what we still want to know about the ancestors of the Tsáchilas, the Chachis, the Awa-Kwaiker, and the many peoples of Western Pichincha that no longer exist. The questions that guided the research are common ones in archaeology, but this case study is not terribly common in some other ways, for it describes a project carried out in a particularly challenging natural environment in which tried-and-true methods had to be abandoned in favor of archaeological improvisation.

Persons interested in archaeology are usually drawn first to the magnificent and awesome monuments of the ancient world—the Egyptian pyramids at Giza, Stonehenge, the lost cities of the Inca or the Maya, the buried terra-cotta army at Xianyang, and so on. Although most archaeologists harbor deep inside them a desire to discover something really extraordinary that will capture the imagination of the world, the fact is that most archaeology tends to capture much less spectacular, but no less important, evidence of the nature of life in ancient times.

I am often asked by interested people what the most exciting find is that I have ever made as an archaeologist, and my answer nearly always disappoints them: a few fragments of charred corn kernels; the 4,000-year-old burial of a dog that had choked to death on a fish; a narrow, deep ditch in the rainforest that is the remnant of an ancient footpath; and tiny pieces of pottery that was made 6,000 years ago by people who were giving up nomadism and learning to farm. Anticipating the disillusionment of the questioner, I quickly explain that I can learn a great deal from any one of those discoveries. Most archaeology is about ancient people, about how they lived and adapted to their surroundings. It is this kind of "humble archaeology," small-scale projects in out-of-the-way places by unknown scientists, that is at the heart of the discipline. Do not be disappointed by it; be amazed that it is possible to find buried bits and traces of ancient human lifeways and that from these seemingly insignificant remnants we can approach an understanding of what life was like hundreds or thousands of years ago.

Despite the possibilities, my primary aim in doing archaeology is not necessarily to learn how to deal with contemporary global problems. I do it mostly because it is exciting and romantic work: I am a "time detective" solving ancient mysteries, traveling to exotic places, always hoping for great surprises, and—perhaps best of all—"playing" in the dirt. I hope that this case study will give students in introductory or intermediate archaeology courses (and perhaps the general public as well) a sense of the thrill and adventure as well as the hard work and tedium.

Archaeology deals with things that are dead and partly disintegrated, with the dust that has accumulated over centuries or millennia. What I will try to do in the following chapters is to breathe life into the story of certain groups of ancient peoples who are mostly unknown to us except through their dusty old tools and structures, traces of which have somehow managed to survive the destructive effects of conquest by nature and other peoples. The artifacts are a means of understanding the people who made them—their challenges, their failures, and their achievements. I find the story to be exciting, and if I tell it well, so will you.

One final introductory comment: I have taken the liberty throughout the book of injecting an occasional personal anecdote about some of the unique tribulations and challenges experienced while carrying out this archaeological project. Some of my colleagues might scoff at these seemingly irrelevant deviations, but they are part of a conscious strategy I have adopted to try to keep the book interesting and intriguing to the reader while being very serious and professional about the project. Even though all archaeologists I know do field research because they love it, for some inexplicable reason we mostly have been trained to write as if archaeology were the most somber, uninteresting job on earth. I hope my writing conveys at least a little of the sense of adventure and pleasure that can be derived from earnest scientific research.

2/The Western Pichincha Project

A FORGOTTEN PART OF ECUADOR

Ecuador is one of the smallest South American countries but contains within its boundaries remarkable geographical diversity, not to mention incredible beauty. The high, rugged Andes Mountains consist of two parallel ranges that run north-south through the country and form something of a backbone (Figure 2.1). This cool, fertile land between the two ranges is referred to as the *sierra* or highlands; farmland, towns, and large cities are found here. Chief among these is the capital city of Quito, which is located in a high valley about 3,000 m (over 9,000 ft.) above sea level and has several snow-capped volcanoes surrounding it. Between the Andes Mountains and the Pacific coast to the west is lower, hotter land that is known simply as "the coast." As one travels the coast from Colombia in the north to Peru in the south, the lowland vegetation changes gradually from lush tropical forest to very dry desert. Finally, the third principal geographic region is found to the east of the Andes. It is the westernmost part of the great Amazonian Basin, the largest area of rivers and tropical forest in the world. Ecuadorians call this third region "the orient," because of its eastward location. Until recently the area was all tropical rainforest, but that is rapidly changing in the face of settlement and agricultural and industrial development.

Ecuadorian geography textbooks always divide the country into these three principal regions, but this often useful division can be a little misleading. Much geographical diversity exists within each region, and people easily forget about the intermediate zones that do not fall cleanly into any of the three categories. These intermediate zones on either side of the Andes are heavily forested and very rugged. They are known in Ecuadorian Spanish as *montaña*, which does not translate into English simply as "mountain" but more accurately as "mountainous jungle."

In modern Ecuador, the montaña areas are practically outside of national awareness. This has been true at least since the coming of the Spanish in 1532, and apparently since the Inca invasion of Ecuador in the middle to late 1400s. Both Incas and Spaniards expressed their aversion to this rugged jungle land, though early Spanish documents indicate that some Incas escaped Spanish dominion by taking refuge on

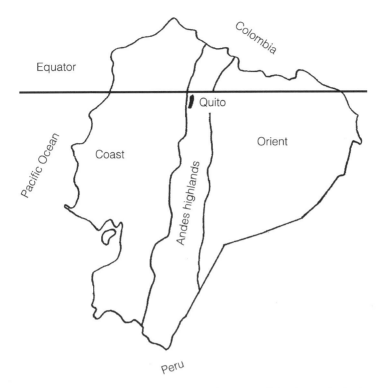

Figure 2.1 Map of Ecuador showing capital city of Quito and the three principal geographical regions

the western flank of the Andes. Early in the 20th century some Ecuadorian revolutionaries hid out in this unexplored wilderness of Pichincha province just west of the capital city of Quito. During the course of our early fieldwork in the same area in the mid-1980s, we heard stories that a leftist rebel group used Western Pichincha as a hideout, and we witnessed more than one small-scale military reconnaissance trying unsuccessfully to ferret them out. Despite the short distance from the city of Quito—a metropolis of a million and a half people with skyscrapers, freeways, shopping malls, and other symbols of modernity and cosmopolitanism—the adjacent western montaña is sparsely inhabited and densely forested, has very few roads, and is an easy place in which to seek refuge if one is hardy.

Since the Spanish conquest in 1532, Western Pichincha has seen the almost complete disappearance of its Native American populations and a gradual colonization over time by *mestizo* peoples. *Mestizo* is a Spanish term referring to people of mixed Spanish and Indian ancestry. Anthropologists recognize many problems inherent in referring to populations in "racial" terms, so I hasten to add that these groups (whether "white," "Spanish," "mestizo," or "Indian") are defined at least as much by cultural traits as biological ones, and that these terms are commonly used (in their Spanish form) by Ecuadorians themselves.

Only in the 1960s did the pace of mestizo settlement of the western montaña begin to accelerate due to rapid population growth throughout Ecuador and the urgent need for more land and resources. This recent migration is altering substantially the natural environment of Western Pichincha. Development has been mostly chaotic and is resulting in large-scale deforestation. Environmental damage is little by little robbing the area of its natural riches and will eventually leave it economically impoverished and perhaps irreversibly polluted. Population pressure and the general poor economic situation of the country will continue to force this anarchical settlement, as is true in many places throughout the world today.

A FLEETING ARCHAEOLOGICAL OPPORTUNITY

A visitor to Western Pichincha a century ago would have been duly impressed by the beauty and severity of the landscape and vegetation, but also would have been hard-pressed to find any evidence of human habitation other than small scattered settlements composed of very small numbers of mestizos. Today the lush tropical forest is rapidly disappearing and the mestizo population is seemingly exploding as new roads provide new options to both rich and poor people in search of land and resources. As the region develops, tourism—nearly unheard of in Western Pichincha as recently as 1990—is booming, and affluent Ecuadorians as well as foreigners from around the world are overrunning the region.

But what did this territory look like five centuries ago? A millennium ago? Four millennia ago? We know there were no Spaniards there before 1532, when Francisco Pizarro and his small army made landfall in northern Peru and ambushed the emperor of the great Inca civilization, bringing to an end that empire and greatly changing the trajectory of thousands of years of Native American cultural development.

From the archaeological perspective, without downplaying the environmental tragedy, this recent colonization of the montaña of Western Pichincha province is a sweet-and-sour turn of events. The settlement of the region—with the road building, forest cutting, and land disturbance—allows for an exploration that otherwise would be nearly impossible to carry out. This ongoing immigration provides us with a fleeting chance to look for and study archaeological sites. As the colonization advances, more and more sites will be destroyed or made inaccessible as they are bulldozed away or covered over by houses, roads, and so on. There really is only a small window of opportunity to carry out such an exploration, so this entire project to some degree could be considered a salvage effort.

In North America, western Europe, and other nations much wealthier than Ecuador, laws are in place to protect archaeological sites or to salvage sites that are in danger of destruction, at least those that are on public lands. Ecuador has similar laws, but they lack almost any power of enforcement, especially in the face of a desperate economic situation. Although officials of the branch of the Ecuadorian government that oversees archaeological research were very supportive of this project, they were not able to aid me in any way to slow down or stop the widespread devastation. In fact, much of the general public accepts without question that such development, chaotic as it seems to be, is good for the country.

Most previous archaeological work in Ecuador (some of which I participated in) had been carried out along the coast or in the sierra. Since I was familiar with the archaeology of both areas and saw some intriguing similarities in early prehistoric pottery between them, it seemed that a study of what was going on in the intermediate region might be very useful. With this kernel of an idea in mind for a project, I took a trip on an old rickety bus deep into Western Pichincha for the first time in 1982 to look at the area. The narrow, winding dirt road snaked down past the towering volcanic peaks of the Andes, some 4,800 m (15,750 ft.) above sea level into the high altitude tropical forest that is known to ecologists as "cloud forest." A landslide interrupted the journey for a couple of hours, and thankfully the bus driver took the hairpin curves more slowly when we got started again. After about four hours of travel from the city of Quito, we made our way through the exceedingly rugged cloud forest and arrived at what remained of the lower elevation subtropical rainforest of Western Pichincha.

I was not a newcomer to Ecuador—having lived, worked, and traveled extensively there for many years before this trip—but I was astounded by the beauty of Western Pichincha and thrilled by the thought of doing "jungle archaeology." I made up my mind that very day to plan an archaeological exploration of the area, even though at the time I was finishing some research on the Pacific coast. In about two years I was back in the area with a contract from the Museum of the Central Bank of Ecuador, the government-run archaeology museum of the country, to conduct a regional archaeological survey of the western part of Pichincha province.

THE WESTERN PICHINCHA RESEARCH REGION

Ecuador is divided into 22 provinces including Pichincha (Figure 2.2). Pichincha is comprised of the capital city of Quito and surrounding valleys in the sierra as well as the western flank of the Andes stretching down to the Pacific coastal plain. The equator runs right through the province, though much of Pichincha enjoys a cool climate due to the high elevation. In order to establish boundaries to the research region, I found it useful to take advantage of natural as well as political borders. Nearly all the northern boundary is formed by the Guayllabamba River, which originates in the highlands around Quito and cuts a deep canyon through the Andes to drain eventually into the Pacific Ocean. The biggest sector of Western Pichincha that was excluded is the city of Santo Domingo de los Colorados and territory to the south and west of that city (where the Tsáchila now live). Consequently, we used the Toachi and Blanco rivers flowing just north of Santo Domingo as the southern and western boundaries.

The area around Santo Domingo is more densely populated than other areas of Western Pichincha, and the land has been substantially modified and intensively cultivated for several decades. It is not an area that was just recently opened to colonization like much of the rest of Western Pichincha. This established a research region of about 5,980 km^2, which is 2% of the entire national territory. Today, there are no cities in the research region, but there are a few small towns and many villages as well as a rapidly growing number of scattered cattle ranches, plantations, lumbering operations, tourist resorts, and even some recently established nature preserves.

As already mentioned, Quito is situated in a large valley between the eastern and western ranges of the Andes. More precisely, it is nestled right up against Pichincha volcano, one of a series of volcanoes that makes up the western Andean range. Pichincha is the highest of these and gives the province its name. The several volcanoes are separated by mountain passes that provide access to the western slopes and the Pacific coast. From the summit of Pichincha or the other volcanoes, one travels westward and downward over very rugged terrain toward the coast. Figure 2.3 is an east-west profile of the Western Pichincha research region from Quito to the coastal plain.

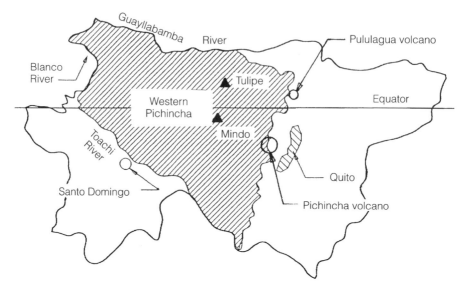

Figure 2.2 Map of Pichincha province showing the Western Pichincha research region

THE NATURAL SETTING

The Western Pichincha research region is primarily the western flank of the Andes Mountains and also includes the piedmont (foothills) and beginning of the coastal plain. This represents a great difference in altitude, topography, climate, and vegetation. In terms of latitude, all of the region is well within the tropics, so the temperature remains quite constant year-round, but it varies considerably depending on elevation. The principal ecological zones of the region are briefly described in the following paragraphs.

The several volcanic peaks, which form a north-south mountain range about 4,800 m (15,750 ft.) above sea level at its highest, are surrounded by cold, humid, windswept meadows above the tree line, which are known in western South America as *páramo*. As one continues down the western páramo, woody vegetation begins to predominate, and by the time one reaches an elevation of 2,900 m (9,500 ft.), one arrives at the high elevation rainforest, known to ecologists as "cloud forest," since the relatively cool air and high humidity combine to form a very cloudy environment. The terrain of the cloud forest is very rugged, with steep-sided mountains and deep river canyons. The yearly temperature average (which barely varies seasonally) is between 12 and 18°C (54–64°F) with average rainfall between 1,000 and 2,000 mm (40–80 in.). Vegetation is very dense, with many species of trees and undergrowth. The agricultural potential of the zone is limited by occasional frosts at the higher altitudes as well as by steep terrain and often poorly developed soils. This ecological zone continues down to about 2,400 m (7,900 ft.) above sea level.

The next major ecological zone, which comprises about two thirds of the entire research region, is known as the subtropical rainforest. This zone continues down through the piedmont (foothills) of the Andes at an elevation of about 500 m (1,640 ft.). Average temperature is 18–24°C (64–75°F), and rainfall amounts are similar to those of the cloud forest. This zone is more propitious for agriculture given the higher temperature and less steep mountains; today this area is favored for growing

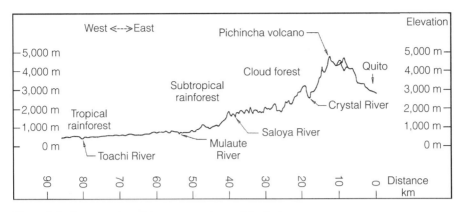

Figure 2.3 Cross-section of the western slope of the Andes

coffee, sugar cane, and corn and for raising cattle, although the soils are poorly developed and would do better with forest cover. Much of this vast zone has been deforested in the past few decades, though there are shrinking areas that are still untouched due to difficulty of access.

The last of the principal ecological zones is the tropical rainforest found below 300 m (985 ft.) above sea level in the westernmost portion of the region. The average temperature here is 24–25°C (75–77°F), with afternoon highs usually around 35°C (95°F). Rainfall is 2,000–4000 mm (80–160 in.). This zone has lost much of its natural forest cover and now has large plantations of African palm and banana as well as cattle pastures and industrial forests (areas planted by lumber companies with fast-growing trees of a single commercially valuable species).

In this mountainous region with very high rainfall, rivers are abundant. About thirty of those rivers originate on the western slope of the Andes and flow westerly into major trunks—the Guayllabamba, the Toachi, and the Blanco. To the northwest (just beyond the boundaries of the research region), these rivers unite to form the Esmeraldas River, which flows to the Pacific Ocean. Due to the ruggedness of the western flank, the rivers are all far too rocky and torrential for navigation until one reaches the low elevation tropical rainforest.

Game animals throughout the region have mostly disappeared in recent decades from overhunting and destruction of habitat, but animals formerly common here were the mountain lion, monkeys, wild pig, tapir, and a number of smaller mammals. Tropical birds, some of the larger of which are still eaten, are tremendously varied and abundant, as are snakes of all sorts, including some venomous species that made our fieldwork somewhat less entertaining than a romp in the woods. The rivers are rich in fishes. Flora of economic use includes many species of excellent hardwood trees as well as American bamboo, many kinds of native fruit trees, and other plants of medicinal, industrial, or food value. Known minerals include gold and salt, neither of which is being exploited on a significant scale today.

Although a brief snapshot of the major climates and resources of the region has just been presented and much more detailed information is available, it is difficult to come by data about the ancient climate of the region. In fact, no climatological study has ever been done in Western Pichincha, and very few have been done throughout western South America. Because some knowledge of ancient climates is essential to a full understanding of ancient populations, I drew upon two studies of pollen cores taken high in the Andes in Colombia and Ecuador (the climatic information from those projects is the only information available that is even remotely close to describing Western Pichincha). Pollen cores are useful in reconstructing ancient climates, since palynologists (geologists or botanists trained in fossil pollen identification) can reconstruct the ancient vegetation of an area based on the pollen samples found. From knowledge of the former plant communities, they can then reconstruct the climate.

While the Pleistocene Epoch (1.8 million to 10,000 years ago) is characterized by major climatic fluctuations resulting in various glacial periods (Ice Ages), the Holocene Epoch (10,000 years ago to the present) has been more stable, with only relatively minor variation. Nonetheless, even minor changes in the climate over centuries or millennia can have a profound impact on the wildlife and human inhabitants. We have yet to discover evidence of human habitation in Western Pichincha before about 3,600 years ago (1600 B.C.), so earlier climatic change is not critical to the present study.

It looks as if the temperature in western South America began decreasing slightly around 3000 B.C. and that both temperature and precipitation have been relatively stable from about 1000 B.C. to the present. It is also believed that the vegetative zones have remained about the same for the last 3,000 years. While much more detailed information would be beneficial, at least this gives us a baseline from which to work.

PREVIOUS ARCHAEOLOGICAL RESEARCH IN THE REGION

Very little archaeology had been performed in Western Pichincha prior to the start of this project. The most significant work was done in the area of the modern village of Tulipe (see Figure 2.2), where local inhabitants showed anthropologist Frank Salomon some "Inca pools" during his visit to the zone in 1978. The pools were subterranean stone-walled ruins that were evidently large baths connected to each other by small stone-lined aqueducts from the nearby river. He and an archaeology colleague performed a preliminary reconnaissance of the site and its environs (Salomon and Erickson 1984) and then turned further research over to specialists at the Central Bank of Ecuador. Holguer Jara (n.d.) led a project to excavate and restore a few of the large underground structures. Analyses were not adequate to resolve the question of whether these baths were built by the Incas or by pre-Inca inhabitants. At least one small structure there appears to be Incan, and the others may be also. Although the final report of that project was finished in 1981, it still has not been published, and perhaps never will be. Even in wealthy countries it is difficult to get full reports of archaeological research published because such technical and scholarly books have a small audience and do not normally make a profit; this is true in Ecuador, too. The unfortunate result is that important knowledge that needs to be widely shared by archaeologists is much harder to come by.

During his work in Tulipe, Jara discovered evidence of a much earlier occupation on a hill adjacent to the pools, and a graduate student from the University of Illinois, John Isaacson, did some excavations at the hilltop site for his Ph.D. research (Isaacson 1987). Isaacson also spent a short time surveying the area around Tulipe for *tolas* (artificial earthen mounds), since there was a very high concentration of them there, and spent a few weeks excavating one of the rectangular platform mounds he located (Isaacson 1982). During our later surveys in Western Pichincha, we mostly shied away from the Tulipe area, since it had already received this attention from colleagues.

Another North American archaeologist, Earl Lubensky, conducted a study of some small round burial mounds on the southern margin of the Western Pichincha region very near the Toachi River in 1979. He produced a brief, preliminary report of that work (Lubensky 1988).

The only other archaeological study was performed by two geographers, who were working with the Ministry of Agriculture to study aerial photographs of the northern Ecuadorian sierra. During the course of their geographical work, it became obvious to them that many archaeological structures were appearing as tiny shadowy patterns in the photographs, so they produced an inventory of those sites (Gondard and López 1983). The structures were primarily of three types—tolas of different shapes and sizes, house circles (the circular imprints on the ground of former house foundations), and forts with concentric stone walls. Although most of their study was in the highlands outside of Western Pichincha, they did include the northeastern corner of Western Pichincha in their book; and there they identified some possible small tolas and house foundations. I studied the same photographs and visited most of the indicated locations but was unable to confirm the existence of any of the mounds or house circles, despite the fact that I traveled with Gondard and López to other sites in the highlands and together we found many other structures that had shown up on the photographs. It is still not clear whether they misidentified some photographic shadows in Western Pichincha or our search to locate those supposed sites was inadequate.

That is the limit of previous archaeological study. The vast majority of Western Pichincha was completely unknown archaeologically, so my project was to be a preliminary regional survey, an initial exploration to get as broad a picture of the ancient history of the region as possible and to establish groundwork (literally and metaphorically) for all future archaeological research there.

3/The Ethnohistory
of Western Pichincha

ETHNOHISTORY

Ethnohistory is that branch of cultural anthropology that attempts to reconstruct the history of cultures or ethnic groups based mostly on documents about those peoples by foreign writers who observed them. In the Americas, with the exception of Mexico and upper Central America, there was no written language in use among the Indians, so our information about their traditional cultures comes primarily from archaeology and from the written records that the Spanish or other Europeans created about those peoples in the decades following contact. To a lesser degree, ethnohistory in this region may also embrace oral tradition handed down over the centuries by the native peoples themselves. Although this project is an archaeological one, it is imperative to try to augment the terribly incomplete and often problematic archaeological record with the written records left to us by the Spanish and, when plausible, by oral tradition.

Ethnohistorical records are ambiguous and cannot always be taken at face value for many reasons. For example, the Spanish explorers tended to be very ethnocentric, which means that they considered their own culture superior to that of the Indians. They often went to great lengths to exaggerate the cultural "deficiencies" of the natives while extolling their own ways. These Spanish writers (usually referred to as "chroniclers") were often missionaries, government bureaucrats, or simply adventurers who had a vested interest in how they told their stories; they tried to write about other cultures and the history of those cultures without the proper education and training for such complex scholarly work. For example, a Catholic priest might exaggerate and distort the religious beliefs and practices of a certain tribe in order to vilify the people as "devil worshipers" and justify his attempts to Christianize them. Furthermore, these writers sometimes had the tendency to fill in missing information with flights of fancy or legends that they gullibly accepted. These and other factors must always be kept in mind when doing ethnohistoric research.

In fact, the difficulties in interpreting both the ethnohistorical record and the archaeological record are so complex that it is extremely useful, when possible, to form hypotheses from each kind of information and test them using the other kind. That is, archaeology and ethnohistory provide checks and balances on each other to ensure that the inferences drawn have a higher probability of being correct. In many archaeological projects, it is not possible to do this, since there is no known historical or cultural continuity between the contemporary residents of a region and the indigenous ones. Fortunately, in the case of Western Pichincha, the Spanish had intermittent contact over nearly three centuries with the native peoples, from the time of first contact until the native cultures mostly disappeared.

Ethnohistory and archaeology are two fields within anthropology, but it is unusual to find persons who are specialized in both. In the case of Western Pichincha, I did not have to try to stumble through an ethnohistoric study, work that I am not qualified to perform on a sophisticated level, because the preliminary research had already been done by a highly respected colleague, Frank Salomon (1997). He completed his ethnohistorical study of Western Pichincha in 1980, but a series of problems in Ecuador meant that the book was not published until 1997, after most of our archaeological fieldwork was finished. Fortunately, Salomon was gracious enough to share the unpublished manuscript and to discuss it with me even before the archaeological project began. The then unpublished book was of great usefulness in planning and carrying out the project. The goal was to draw upon both archaeological and ethnohistorical data to learn as much as possible about the pre-Hispanic inhabitants of Western Pichincha.

The following sections summarize very briefly the ethnohistorical information about the various groups of Native Americans of the research region. This is based mostly but not entirely on Salomon's studies. In Chapter 9 of this book, an attempt is made to combine this knowledge with that obtained through our archaeological research in order to draw some preliminary conclusions. Figure 3.1 indicates the approximate locations in and around Western Pichincha of the ethnic groups described here as well as a few others in the area.

THE YUMBOS[1]

The Spanish priest and chronicler Miguel Cabello Balboa was named "Vicar of the province of Yumbos" in 1577, a few decades after first contact between the Spanish and Andean peoples in 1532. Cabello Balboa was one of the very few chroniclers in the early Spanish period who actually traveled in Western Pichincha so his writings, unlike those of certain others, were often based on firsthand information rather than hearsay. Cabello Balboa informs us of the territory of the principal Indians of Western Pichincha, the Yumbos, by referring in a somewhat vague manner to neighboring tribes on all sides, tribes that are associated with certain geographic zones. Originally he declared that the "Yumbo Nation" extended all the way from the peaks of the Andes just west of Quito to the coastal plain of northwestern Ecuador. He then went on to clarify that this large territory was actually divided into two nations, with the Yumbos living at the higher elevations, that is, on the western flank of the Andes, and a nation of people known as Niguas[2] living west of the Yumbos nearer the Pacific Ocean (Cabello Balboa 1945 [1579?]:62–63).

---

[1]Pronounced with an English long "u" (as in tube) and long "o" (as in go): YUM-bohs.
[2]Pronounced NEE-gwahs.

Figure 3.1 Map of Ecuador showing known pre-Hispanic indigenous groups in and around Western Pichincha

Another chronicler, one who did not have firsthand knowledge of the Yumbos, wrote the following description of them in 1553:

> From here [the village of Panzaleo] one takes a road that goes to the mountains of the Yumbos, in which there are some towns whose natives are not very servile as are the Indians around Quito, nor are they very subdued; on the contrary they are more unruly and arrogant. This comes from living in such rough terrain which, due to the warmth and fertility, is well endowed with resources. They also worship the sun and are similar in their customs and concerns to their neighbors, because they were subjugated by the great Topa Inca Yupanqui and by Huayna Capac, his son. . . . (Cieza de León 1962 [1553]:132–133, excerpt translated by Lippi)

From this brief excerpt, one gets a sense of the 16th century writing style punctuated with value judgments. Topa Inca Yupanqui and Huayna Capac were two Inca emperors before the arrival of the Spanish, so the narrative, if it is correct, implies that the Yumbos were conquered by the Inca, a great militaristic empire that expanded northward from southern Peru during the 1400s. There is also mention made of the rich resources of Yumbo country. From other sources we know that the Yumbos raised subtropical and tropical foods and plants—especially cotton, manioc (or cassava, a starchy root crop that is a staple throughout much of tropical America), corn, chili peppers, various fruits, sweet potatoes, incense, and rubber—and they also mined gold and salt. These commodities were traded to the various Andean ethnic groups living in large agricultural towns around Quito and neighboring sierra valleys.

Cieza de León refers to the "unruly" manner of the Yumbos. In the eyes of the Spanish conquerors, any peoples that resisted domination were labeled as "wild," "savages," or "cannibals" and considered inferior because of their reluctance to give up their sovereignty and submit to foreign masters.[3]

Salomon (1997:18–19) has been able to determine that regular exchange between the Yumbos and the highland Indians was very important for both economies and that this interregional trade was often formalized through alliances, intermarriage, and foot travel between the highlands and the montaña of Western Pichincha. An additional fact discovered by Salomon is the existence of a network of "roads" (actually they were footpaths) that connected various parts of Yumbo country with the sierra. The principal roads are described in early Spanish documents, and the Indian villages they connected are listed. This gives us the names and approximate location of certain villages, leaving it to the archaeologist to confirm their existence and find their precise location.

Salomon (1997:33–34) was able to glean from other sources something about Yumbo architecture and dress. Within a certain locality, small houses surrounded by fields were clustered together to form what can only loosely be called "towns." The houses were built of palm trunks and the roofs were covered with large leaves. It is said that each house was far enough from the neighboring ones that they could barely be seen. This allowed for small fields around each house, suggesting the use of slash-and-burn cultivation, which is the typical form of horticulture in forested areas. Figure 3.2 shows an area of modern farmsteads in the region, and Figure 3.3 is a close-up of one of the few remaining traditional houses of Western Pichincha; both the settlement pattern and the house may be similar to what the Yumbos used many centuries ago. The Yumbos typically wore little dress but often used body paint, and the men frequently used a bright red paint in their hair (similar to the Tsáchilas).

Beyond this, not very much is known of the Yumbos. It is not known if Yumbos were a single nation of people or several similar, neighboring nations. If they were more than one nation, it is uncertain whether they were linked by any political system or by close social or religious ties. We do not know whether they all spoke the same language or a variety of closely related languages. There is evidence, however, based on Spanish commentary and some of the place names that have survived to modern times, that the Yumbo language or languages belonged to a language family known as Barbacoan, which in turn belongs to a language stock called Macro-Chibchan, which is quite widespread in northwestern South America and Central America. This language was quite distinct from the Inca language, Quechua, which is still very widely spoken by Andean and upper Amazonian Indians in South America today.

THE NIGUAS

The second major indigenous group of Western Pichincha referred to by Cabello Balboa is the Niguas. We know from him that they lived to the west of the Yumbos and at a lower elevation all the way to the north Pacific coast, but the boundary between the two nations cannot be determined by the ethnohistoric record.

---

[3]It is interesting that the Inca conquerors made similar references to the Yumbos a few decades earlier, as will be seen in a later section.

Figure 3.2 Dispersed houses and gardens in a small valley of Western Pichincha. This modern settlement pattern may be similar to the ancient pattern of the Yumbos.

Figure 3.3 One of the last remaining native-type houses (called a "barbacoa") in Western Pichincha

In trying to figure out who the Niguas were, allow me to stray briefly onto a tangent. In the mid- to late 1970s when I was involved in archaeological projects on the south Ecuadorian coast, I was repeatedly annoyed by insect infestations in the soles of my feet and under my toenails. Small female fleas of the species *Sarcopsylla penetrans* burrowed into my feet to lay their eggs. The egg cysts itched horribly. On the advice of local inhabitants, I opened the small wounds and cleaned out the cysts with a sterilized needle and rubbing alcohol. My poor feet seemed to hold the distinction of "most desirable" by the fleas in one village, where I became known to the locals as "the nigua man."

Nigua is the local name for these pests, which brings me back to the Nigua Indians. While it may be a coincidence that the name for native inhabitants of the northwest coast of Ecuador and this bothersome flea is the same, I think it more likely that one usage gave rise to the other. It may have been that the tradition of the Nigua Indians as fierce and persistent carried over and inspired more recent mestizos to refer to the fleas by the same name. Conversely, maybe enemies of the native inhabitants of the northwest coast were named after the flea. Either way, I consider *Nigua* a possibly pejorative term, and can only wonder what those ancient peoples called themselves.

Salomon (1997:22, 32) found information he interpreted to mean that there were two villages near the Yumbo-Nigua ethnic boundary, Bolaniguas in the north and Cocaniguas in the south, as well as an uninhabited buffer zone between the two "nations." This intriguing historical datum is testable archaeologically, and some effort has been made to locate those two "lost villages," as will be seen in Chapter 7.

A Spanish ethnohistorian, Josefina Palop Martínez (1986:241), has studied documents relating to the Niguas and has tried to determine their exact territory and language. Regarding the language they spoke, she believes it was the same as the Yumbo language, judging by a transcribed (recopied) handwritten document from the 1600s. Salomon read the same document and interpreted one word differently, leading him to believe that the Nigua language differed from the Yumbo. What the discrepancy comes down to is deciphering one letter in one word. If the letter is an "m," then Palop Martínez is correct; if it is a "t," then Salomon is correct. Cabello Balboa (1945 [1579?]:62–63) informs us that the Niguas and Yumbos are sometimes all called Yumbos, but that the Niguas have their own language, customs, and dress. This statement, if it can be taken literally, supports Salomon's interpretation. Such are the perils of ethnohistoric research.

In the introduction to this book, I mentioned two other tribes besides the Tsáchila who still live in northwestern Ecuador. One is the Awa-Kwaiker, about whose origin very little is known, though they may very well have been "Niguas." The other nation is popularly known today as the Cayapas, though they refer to themselves as the Chachi. They live today on the forested coastal plain of Esmeraldas province, to the north of the Western Pichincha research region. Some Ecuadorian scholars have concluded that the Chachi are the surviving descendants of the Niguas, while others have pointed to the oral tradition of the Chachi, which claims that their homeland originally was in the Andean highlands and that they migrated to the coastal lowlands to escape invaders—either the Incas or, somewhat later, the Spanish. Since Chachi territory is outside the Western Pichincha region, we were not able to address that issue in our project. However, another archaeological project directed by Warren DeBoer (1995) surveyed the Chachi territory and found quite clear evidence, in the form of changes in the pottery tradition, that the Chachis were late migrants into the Nigua region. Here is an instance where the archaeological record provides fairly clear support for the validity (or at least partial validity) of native oral tradition.

As was true with the Yumbos, it is not yet possible, based on the known Spanish records, to determine whether the Niguas were a single homogeneous nation or several similar nations that lived in the same general area. When Spanish missionaries began living and working among the Niguas in the late 1500s, they wrote of several different named ethnic groups, but they often arbitrarily named these "tribes" after the local village leader rather than by actual ethnic labels, so this only confuses the matter of determining just who were the Niguas.

THE CAMPACES, "COLORADOS," AND TSÁCHILAS

According to Cabello Balboa (1945 [1579?]:15), the Campaces were the native inhabitants of an extensive territory between the Andes Mountains and the Pacific Ocean to the south of Nigua territory. The following citation raises some interesting points about these people:

> The Campaces, people who inhabit those mountains that we spoke about, are the most warlike of that area. They and only they were feared by the Negroes that entered there, as we will explain later. These are not people who recognize a principal chief; on the contrary all is confusion, although they do unite militarily against any common enemy. They are superstitious and fortunetellers and they look to soothsayers. (Cabello Balboa 1945 [1579?]:15, excerpt translated by Lippi)

The "Negroes" mentioned here could be a relatively dark-skinned native tribe or, more likely, escaped African slaves who fled into the interior of Ecuador in the 1500s and whose descendants are very numerous today in the north coastal province of Esmeraldas.

Spaniards and other Europeans considered Indians who lived in egalitarian societies without clearly established chiefs or kings to be inferior, so the statement that the Campaces do not live under a principal chief but in confusion becomes understandable from the European perspective of the 16th century. This European prejudice is reflected in the English word *anarchy,* which literally means "without government or rule," and is often used as a synonym for chaos or utter confusion. Anthropologists, on the other hand, have studied egalitarian societies for over a century and understand that the lack of centralized authority in small-scale societies does not at all imply chaos or confusion.

Our knowledge of the Campaces is extremely limited. Because of their alleged settlement in the montaña and coastal plain south of the Yumbos and Niguas, some scholars have concluded that the Tsáchila, who also live today immediately south of former Yumbo territory, are the modern descendants of the Campaces. I find the geographic descriptions of their territory to be so vague as to render this conclusion dubious. Tsáchila oral tradition may contradict this conclusion as well. The Tsáchila worshipped volcano deities who lived in the Andean highlands east of their present territory. This fact has been used to argue that they may have formerly lived in the sierra and migrated into the montaña in recent centuries.

There are a number of confusing references to "Colorados" in a variety of Spanish documents. Various scholars have assumed for the most part that "Colorado" refers to Tsáchila, because such is the case today in modern Ecuador. However, my own reading of some of those documents suggests that the Spanish referred to any montaña Indians who used annatto-based red paint extensively as "Colorados," but the use of annatto by tropical forest Indians was widespread from parts of Central America to Brazil. So it is probably wrong to assume that the term *Colorado* in early texts refers specifically to the Tsáchila; more likely, it was a generic term that Spaniards used to refer to almost any tropical forest Indians.

Salomon (1997:95–96), based on his extensive review of ethnohistoric documents for the region and time period, has his own hypothesis on Tsáchila origins. He believes the Tsáchila may have originated as a distinct ethnic group during the 17th or 18th century as remnant Yumbo peoples in the southern sector of Western Pichincha came together in the face of plummeting population and increasing Spanish dominance. In other words, the Tsáchila may have come into existence as a tribe from the fusion of the scattered remains of various Yumbo or related peoples.

The story is even more complicated than this if we consider again Tsáchila oral tradition. The Tsáchila tell of their former occupation of a large settlement known as Cocaniguas (the same name Salomon came across in his archival studies) and their abandonment of that town due to an epidemic. A prominent businessman and politician in the city of Santo Domingo took it upon himself to try to find this "lost town" of the Tsáchila and even wrote a book about his adventures (Velástegui 1989). When he found grinding stones and some small knolls he mistook for burial mounds near the Cocaniguas River, he declared that he had found the ancient capital of the Tsáchila. My crew and I subsequently visited the same site and we found a few scattered artifacts, as can be found practically anywhere in the region, but no evidence of the lost town. Nevertheless, based on our own studies of ethnohistoric documents, oral reports by contemporary settlers, and old maps, I believe that Velástegui was looking in the right area.

According to the oral tradition that Velasteguí recounts, a man named Joaquín Zaracay, who was purportedly born around 1840, served as the last chief of Cocaniguas; he died in 1942, long after the Tsáchila moved to the Santo Domingo area. If that story is reliable, the abandonment of Cocaniguas could have been as recent as the mid- to late 1800s. It might seem unlikely that such an important settlement of a relatively recent date would be unknown today, but the fact is that the dense montaña area of Cocaniguas was completely uninhabited in recent times until the 1960s, and even today is only very sparsely inhabited. It would have been easy for a settlement to be rapidly overgrown and "lost" within just a few decades.

THE CARANQUIS

To the north of Quito in the Andean highlands, there is abundant archaeological and historical information on the existence of four major chiefdoms and some minor ones that are often known collectively as the Caranquis or Caras. These various nations formed a military alliance against Inca incursion and were able to hold off the great Inca army for many years before finally suffering a devastating defeat. The final Inca victory came on the shores of a lake that to this day is known by its Inca term, *Yaguarcocha,* which means "lake of blood," since thousands of Caranquis were slaughtered and thrown in the lake as the angry Incas finally exacted revenge for such prolonged resistance.

Inca domination of the various Caranqui nations meant some cultural homogenization as well as the adoption of a northern dialect of the Inca language, Quichua, which is still widely spoken today by the descendants of the Caranqui. Among these descendants are such well-known ethnic groups in northern Ecuador as the Otavalo and the Cayambe.

For our purposes here, the most relevant fact about the Caranquis is that prior to the Inca invasion, they built great earthen mounds (called *tolas* in Ecuador), dozens of which still exist today in the highlands. These mounds were mostly of two types. One type, often called a pyramid or platform mound, is usually a rectangular mound with a flat top, often with one or two long ramps leading up to the platform. It is believed that the Caranqui chiefs lived atop these mounds and that the mounds themselves served as great public monuments. In addition to the platform mounds, there were also large round or sometimes nearly conical mounds, which were burial mounds for the elites. This mound-building custom is relevant, since we found very similar earthen mounds within Western Pichincha, suggesting some sort of cultural or historical link between the two regions.[4]

THE INCA INVASION

Reference has already been made to the expansion of the Inca Empire out of southern Peru and the eventual conquest during the late 1400s of the Caranquis in Ecuador's northern Andes. The ethnohistoric literature even gives us some details about the names of the commanders, the sequence of events, the intrigues and battles, and so on. The Incas were highland peoples, and the Andes Mountains formed the backbone of their enormous empire. In Peru and northern Chile, where the coastal lowlands are desert rather than tropical forest, they also expanded their hegemony over many coastal chiefdoms and states. However, Inca attempts to expand into tropical forest areas were usually unsuccessful in what was to them a very hostile, unfamiliar environment and against the alleged ferocity of the jungle inhabitants, whose warfare was more guerilla-like than the warfare to which the Incas were accustomed.

In what is today Ecuador, the Incas made incursions into the Pacific coastal lowlands, including an ill-fated expedition to an island in the Gulf of Guayaquil, where Inca troops were slaughtered while being ferried to the mainland by a local tribe. Beyond this scant information, it was generally assumed that the Incas were no more enthusiastic or successful at dominating western Ecuadorian nations than they were in other parts of the moist tropical lowlands of South America.

Salomon (1997:23–26) obtained data that led him to draw three conclusions about the Incas in Western Pichincha. First, there was an oral tradition written down by Cabello Balboa that indicated that the Yumbos were indeed conquered by Guanca Auqui, a brother of the Inca emperor. It is worth including the excerpt here, as it demonstrates a rather condescending attitude the Incas apparently maintained toward the Yumbos, perhaps because they were not so easy to bring under control:

---

[4]While there is no known or hypothesized historical connection, it is interesting that the late pre-European "Mississippian Period" in the eastern United States also witnessed the building of platform and burial mounds of similar structure and functions.

Guanca Auqui . . . made trips against the province of Yumbos; and having conquered and subjugated those naked peoples and seeing their poverty and little worth, they returned to Quito. (Cabello Balboa 1951 [1586]:437–438; translated by Lippi)

Secondly, unlike other regions conquered by the Incas and incorporated into their well-organized administrative system, it appears that the Yumbos remained in an anomalous position. They were not divided into the usual Inca administrative units, and they apparently did not pay tribute to the Inca. This suggests that there may have been a nominal military conquest but that the traditional economic system of the Yumbos was not substantially altered. Thirdly, Salomon found evidence that some Incas sought refuge in Western Pichincha following the Spanish conquest.

There is also mention in Spanish documents of two "royal highways" through Western Pichincha. Spaniards normally referred to important Inca roads by the Spanish or Quichua equivalent of "royal highway." The Incas had been exceptional road builders throughout their empire, and the existence of Inca roads into Western Pichincha implies military conquest and/or regular trading relations.

THE SPANISH COLONIAL PERIOD

The Spanish Colonial Period nominally began in 1532, with the capture and execution in northern Peru of the Inca emperor Atahualpa by Francisco Pizarro, and ended in 1822 with Ecuadorian independence from Spain (and Colombia). Most of the ethnohistoric information Salomon obtained about the Yumbos, Niguas, and other nations refers to this period when the Spaniards attempted to incorporate Western Pichincha into their New World empire. Many of the details of Salomon's study are not relevant here, but enough background will be given to lay the groundwork for the archaeological study that follows.

Various references from the mid-1500s indicate that there were rebellions or uprisings among the Yumbos and Niguas, resulting in the fairly early perception on the part of the Spanish that these montaña Indians were hostile and treacherous. One way for the Spanish government to reward those who participated in the exploration and conquest of the Americas was to give them large land concessions, called *encomiendas* in Spanish. When the encomiendas were made in Pichincha, it was common practice for a Spaniard to be given control over a highland district including one or two towns as well as a Yumbo settlement in the montaña. Salomon (1997:30) noted this tendency and inferred that it probably reflected a long-time economic relationship that had existed between certain highland and montaña communities, a practice that the Spanish chose to continue.

These land grants usually did not involve much Spanish intervention in Western Pichincha, since the grantees all preferred to live and work in the highlands, but a much higher impact invasion by Spaniards began in 1570 with the establishment of Catholic missionary districts. Much of the northern part of Western Pichincha was assigned to priests and friars of the Roman Catholic Mercedarian Order, while the southern half of the region was taken over by the Dominican Order. A handful of settlements in between the two orders was under the jurisdiction of regular Catholic clergy. The Society of Jesus (Jesuit Order) gained control over only the extreme northeastern corner of Western Pichincha, so their involvement in the region was very slight. The primary goal of these missionaries was to "save souls" by converting "heathens" to Christianity. Their usual procedures were the following: to learn the local Indian language, to make the Indians honor the Sabbath, to take censuses, to build churches, and to stamp out what the Church considered sexual promiscuity and witchcraft.

The matter of censuses is an important one, since it is well known that the coming of the Europeans to America brought tremendous loss of life among the Native Americans. The causes were many, but the unintentional importation of Old World infectious diseases—smallpox, measles, typhus fever, bubonic plague, influenza, and many others—had the most significant impact throughout the hemisphere. A few other factors precipitated by Spaniards and other Europeans in this massive native depopulation of the Americas included warfare against the invaders, genocide, loss of subsistence, and brutal slavery imposed upon the Indians.

Various documents provided by the missionaries and others allow us to reconstruct part of the population history of the Western Pichincha native inhabitants. As with other ethnohistoric research, there is a fair amount of error and uncertainty in the data that survive, but cross-checking when possible and searching for some consistency in the data give us some confidence that the numbers are reasonably accurate and complete. I compiled all the data I could find, much of it gathered originally by Salomon (1997), but some from other sources, and then I constructed a population table for the entire Western Pichincha region. Spanish censuses often counted the number of tribute-payers rather than the whole population for a settlement or area. For the most part, adult men were the tribute-payers, and the ratio of tribute-payers to the whole population was fairly consistent throughout the Andes: about 1:3.5. So in those cases where only the tribute-paying numbers were given, it is possible to estimate the total population with some confidence.

This matter of extrapolating the population backward in time from fairly reliable numbers is complex and relies on a number of assumptions. I made the extrapolation in five different ways, each based on a different assumption I thought reasonable, and each of the five estimates falls within the range of 22,000 to 30,000 Yumbo inhabitants. Allow me to state in the briefest way how a couple of those estimates work (more detail concerning the five different calculations is summarized in a paper I presented at an archaeological conference; see Lippi 2001).

One estimate starts with the fairly reliable census figures from the early 1600s and late 1500s and works backward, estimating the rate of population decline based on what is known of the major Old World epidemics that swept through Ecuador. Records of epidemics are precise enough to allow us to estimate when particular diseases struck, how virulent (deadly) they were, and when they passed. I used comparable figures from other parts of the Americas and estimated a yearly population decline of 2% during nonepidemic years and 6% for epidemic years. The final estimate going back to 1524, the year that the first smallpox epidemic hit South America, was close to 24,000 people, which I consider the baseline (or final precontact) population. The resulting numbers from this particular method of calculation are summarized in Table 3.1. This table is divided into time segments based on the census counts that were available and the years of the start and finish of major epidemics. Note that population decline slowed considerably as the overall population approached zero and the century-long series of epidemics passed. By the 1600s, the rate of depopulation had fallen to less than 1% per year. As expected, the high rate of depopulation occurred early on.

TABLE 3.1 ESTIMATE OF BASELINE YUMBO POPULATION*

Year	Yumbo Population	Average Depopulation Rate/Year	Population Density	Overall Depopulation
1900	0	not applicable	0	100%
1780	944	0.9%	0.2	96%
1649	3,000	0.4%	0.7	87%
1591	3,752	6%	0.9	84%
1582	6,123	6%	1.5	74%
1560	9,350	6%	2.2	61%
1558	9,950	2%	2.4	58%
1546	12,425	6%	3.0	48%
1541	15,915	2%	3.8	33%
1533	18,330	6%	4.4	23%
1532	19,500	2%	4.6	18%
1527	21,140	6%	5.0	12%
1524	23,925		5.7	

*Assuming depopulation rates for epidemic and nonepidemic years and working backward from censuses

A completely different type of population estimate is based on ecological rea-soning. I looked around South America for population densities of native peoples in recent times living with traditional technology in roughly similar ecological niches. Based on the figures available, I estimated Yumbo population density prior to European contact and the onset of Old World epidemics to be approximately $7/km^2$. Given a total surface area of Yumbo territory of 4,200 km^2 (based on information summarized in Chapter 9), I estimated the total population at the time of first contact at about 29,400 people. As I said earlier, these and three other methods of calculation all gave estimates between 22,000 and 30,000, for which I have somewhat arbitrar-ily chosen 25,000 as a reasonable ballpark estimate.

This question of population size and density is not simply a matter of curiosity. For one thing, the complexity of sociopolitical organization is somewhat dependent on population, and for another, it would be valuable to know how many Native Americans lived in the tropical forests of Western Pichincha apparently without causing significant environmental degradation. The more we know about the size of the Indian nations, the more we know about their adaptation and social complexity. Most any anthropologist will affirm that the population density and overall size of a society and the abundance of vital natural resources go a long way toward influenc-ing to what degree that society will develop status differences, centralized govern-ment, nonreciprocal exchange of goods, and so on. Knowing the population of the Yumbos will eventually help us a great deal in understanding their cultural evolution.

By 1900 there were virtually no identifiable indigenous peoples left in Western Pichincha. What happened to them? Undoubtedly, many of them died from infec-tious disease, warfare and rebellions against the Spanish, and other causes. It is known that some of them avoided censuses and Spanish domination by moving far-ther and farther from centers of Spanish control. Ultimately, those that survived and remained in the region probably became less and less identifiable as native peoples through the processes of acculturation and intermarriage with the Spanish. To what extent their extinction was biological and to what extent it was cultural cannot yet be determined with confidence. The Tsáchila, the Chachi, and the Awa-Kwaiker are the only suspected survivors of the Yumbos and Niguas, and they no longer live within the research region designated as Western Pichincha.

One final note about the Spanish Colonial Period: There were a few attempts by the Spanish to construct usable roads through Western Pichincha. Many of these involved forced Indian labor and forced relocation of Indian villages so they would be close to the newly built roads. In the end, all of these attempts to build roads through the rugged terrain of cloud forest and rainforest of western Pichincha failed. It was not until the 20th century that significant road building succeeded, and even then a few projects failed.

THE 19TH AND 20TH CENTURIES

Throughout the colonial period and into the independence period of the last two centuries, a few attempts to incorporate Western Pichincha into the national economy failed, mostly due to the lack of reliable roads and the general hardships involved in exploiting this isolated, rugged region. Although there is occasional mention of surviving Indian customs or individuals in the 1800s, the Yumbo and Nigua nations seem no longer to exist by the beginning of Ecuadorian independence in 1822. The population of native peoples as well as recent colonists continued to decline until reaching its nadir around 1900. Many Indian villages and Catholic missions were abandoned by that time, and the land reclaimed by the tropical forest.

In each of two villages where we spent a lot of time, we met a very old individual who is said to have been one of the last descendants of the Yumbos of that area. Both were purported to be over 100 years old, though we could not confirm that. Our interviews with both of them were fruitless because of their advanced age and declining memory. They have both passed away now.

Road building became more vigorous in the 20th century. A gravel road through the southern part of Western Pichincha was completed in 1933 and others farther north in the 1960s. With these roads, the modern recolonization of the region became feasible. Some of the towns and villages that survived from earlier times with small populations began to grow starting in the 1960s, and much of the tropical forest around them was cut down and replaced by pasture land. The higher elevation cloud forest on the eastern end of the research region, due to its extreme ruggedness, still has not been substantially altered, though that will change gradually with continued road building and immigration.

A major asphalt east-west highway all the way through Western Pichincha, constructed during the 1980s and opened in the 1990s, has led to a massive migration into the region in recent years. Less and less tropical forest survives, and more and more archaeological sites are being destroyed, as the land is coming under modern exploitation. The Yumbos and Niguas are long gone, and apparently so is their knowledge of how to live in this delicate habitat. Perhaps archaeology can serve to recover a little of that valuable knowledge. Now that this brief ethnohistorical summary of Western Pichincha has been presented, it is time to move on to the archaeological project.

4/Looking for Sites
in All the Right Places

THE RATIONALE FOR A REGIONAL SURVEY

An archaeological survey is the systematic search for sites. Recent and newly emerging technology—including detailed photography from earth orbit, thermal infrared imagery, ground-penetrating radar, and other remote-sensing devices—has already begun to revolutionize how surveying is done. Nonetheless, these methods are often not available or affordable, nor are they always appropriate. When all is said and done, the classic method of pedestrian surveying—systematically walking over the territory looking for artifacts and features on the surface—remains the most common method of finding sites and was utilized to the extent possible in Western Pichincha.

Prior to the 1960s, surveying was frequently little more than a prelude to excavation. Since that time, surveying, especially of large regions, has emerged as an extremely valuable strategy by itself. Regional surveys provide important data about various kinds of sites in differing habitats throughout a territory, whereas excavations provide detailed data on a single site within a single niche. Moreover, excavating is extremely painstaking, slow, labor-intensive, and costly compared to pedestrian surveying. While excavations certainly provide very useful kinds of information, so do surveys. Among the goals of regional surveys one can list studies of settlement patterns, area population, economic adaptations to natural environments, ethnic boundaries, and human migration patterns, among other important facts.

There are also conservation considerations: sooner or later archaeology students learn the maxim "To excavate a site is to destroy it." Whereas excavation of even a small portion of a site results in the destruction of context and association in the site, surveying and the collection only of surface artifacts are much less destructive of the archaeological record. Modern archaeology has turned more and more from the excavation of sites to their preservation. As the human population continues to grow rapidly and as development threatens an ever-increasing number of sites throughout the world, surveying presents itself as an effective strategy by which to salvage a significant portion of the vanishing archaeological record.

In Ecuador prior to the Western Pichincha Project, surveying had been done only on a much smaller scale, usually within a locality of several square kilometers, but not across an entire region of the country. Choosing to do a regional survey across a territory that was unexplored archaeologically yet was bounded both to the east and the west by known archaeological complexes seemed a reasonable strategy to pursue. Not only could such a project open up a new region to study, but it could also make connections between disparate cultures and begin to form a broader, more complete picture of prehistory in that part of the continent.

WESTERN PICHINCHA—A SURVEYOR'S HELL?

Accessibility was the first formidable problem encountered as the project got underway. The landscape, particularly of the cloud forest, is extremely rugged; the forest cover throughout many sectors of the region is very dense; and roads are few and far between. Getting into the region and then moving around freely within it were difficult undertakings. During the course of the project, the road problem improved due to the construction of a major highway through the region and the gradual opening up of various secondary roads. This improved access considerably. For example, whereas it used to take four hours to travel by a very bad road from Quito to Mindo, where we spent several months excavating a site, after the new paved highway was constructed, Mindo could be reached comfortably in less than two hours. Nonetheless, during the early years of the project, travel into and through the research region was mostly very slow and restricted.

Having a four-wheel-drive vehicle in decent condition was another prerequisite for travel in the area that turned out to be quite a challenge. For the first two years of the project, I had to use my own vehicle, an old Nissan Patrol (an early, rustic prototype of today's SUVs). The Patrol was in poor condition but was our only means of travel within the region. The vehicle was constantly breaking down on us, and we lost a lot of field time because of it. I tallied more than thirty flat tires before losing count, and on eight occasions the rear axle springs broke and had to be replaced, which should give the reader some indication of the roughness of the roads. We had many other breakdowns, including a gasoline tank that leaked like a sieve and brakes that failed on a hairpin mountain curve, much to our dismay. In subsequent field seasons, we tried to rent a reliable vehicle, but that was always very costly and something of a crapshoot.

While driving around Western Pichincha, we had to negotiate countless "bridges" (and I use the term loosely). Although the bridges on the few main roads were well-built concrete bridges, once we got off the main roads, we encountered bridges that were improvised by the local inhabitants, most of whom did not have motor vehicles and built bridges primarily for pedestrians and horses. The simplest bridges comprised three or four large trees that were felled and positioned to straddle a stream. Sometimes a few wooden planks were laid over the tree trunks, and other times we simply had to steer the vehicle carefully to stay on the trunks. At the opposite extreme were fairly elaborate suspension bridges. These swayed noticeably under the weight of our vehicle and sagged in a very disconcerting manner. One large suspension bridge had originally been built with six huge steel cables, three on each side, from which the bridge was suspended. When a gravel quarry was opened in the area, large dump trucks began using the bridge and strained it so much that only two of the six cables remained.

Perhaps the most interesting bridge was a very nice concrete bridge built in a village that was in a contested part of Western Pichincha; the territory was claimed by both Pichincha and Esmeraldas provinces. Each provincial government in turn tried to lure the villagers to identify with their province through building projects. One province built a one-room school, and the other built a bridge. What was odd about this bridge was that there was no vehicle road into the village, only a narrow horse trail that led directly to this wide, two-lane concrete bridge.

The actual archaeological surveying was done on foot. Often it was pleasant to leave the rattletrap vehicle and bumpy roads and to take off walking along jungle paths. On only one occasion did we borrow a couple of horses to take us into a particularly remote region of forest. Despite the countless footpaths that crisscrossed different sectors of Western Pichincha, the overwhelming majority of the research region, in terms of surface area, could not be directly accessed for pedestrian survey. Following roads and trails necessarily limited the survey to very restricted linear transects, as will be discussed more in the text that follows.

Visibility of the ground surface was the second major difficulty in the pedestrian survey, which relies on visual inspection of the ground for surface artifacts or structures. The dense vegetation severely limited artifact or structure visibility. The ground cover over much of the region is rainforest of one type or another, with dense undergrowth. In areas where the forest has been cleared, one most commonly finds pastureland with high, dense, tropical grasses. Even in the agricultural areas, such as in sugarcane fields and banana or African palm plantations, the soil around the plants and trees is not cultivated, and there is dense weed growth. Large structures, such as tolas, are visible in pastures or other cleared areas, but small structures and surface artifacts are hidden. Only during the very short time that deforestation is in process and before herding or agriculture has gained a foothold—that is, while the terrain is recently cleared—is it feasible to survey the land away from roads and trails. The discovery of such clearings at the right time was due to a combination of perseverance and luck. Figure 4.1 illustrates typical cloud forest vegetation on either side of a barely visible footpath; even a lost city would be difficult to find under such conditions.

The Ecuadorian Air Force has an inventory of aerial photographs of virtually all of Western Pichincha, and I was able to study those at the Military Geographic Institute in Quito. Although I have some training in inspecting aerial photographs with a stereoscope (an optical device similar to a child's ViewMaster™ that creates the illusion of three-dimensional viewing), the photographs were not useful because of the dense vegetation.

Even when plant cover was sparse or absent, surface artifacts were not always visible because of volcanic activity in the area. The occasional eruption of a few nearby Andean volcanoes over the millennia has buried much of the surface under tephra (volcanic ash, sand, and pumice stone). When it comes to excavations, this stratigraphy of volcanic sediments is actually advantageous, since the ash layers serve as dividing layers of known age. However, the most recent major ashfall (not including two minor ashfalls in 1999) took place in 1660, when Pichincha volcano immediately west of Quito erupted and covered much of Western Pichincha with several centimeters of ash. That means that even the latest pre-Hispanic (pre-1532) occupations in the region, unless the sediments have been eroded or otherwise

Figure 4.1 Barely visible footpath (bottom center) through cloud forest vegetation

disturbed, are covered over. This series of ashfalls over time also means that early pre-Hispanic sites are often very deeply buried. For example, a series of ashfalls in the first millennium A.D. deposited as much as 2 m (6½ ft.) of ash in some areas of Western Pichincha, so any sites prior to that are very difficult to find.

The third and final major impediment to the surveying of Western Pichincha was the deficiency of maps of the region, which in turn made it difficult to determine the precise location of many sites that were discovered. Although the Military Geographic Institute has worked for decades to produce detailed topographic maps of all of Ecuador, such maps for the eastern half of Western Pichincha were out of date with regard to villages and roads and occasionally slightly unreliable; no topographic maps even existed for the western half of the region. For the western half, topographic maps eventually became available during the later seasons of fieldwork, but all the early work was done without the benefit of such maps. Instead, we relied upon planimetric maps, which lack the topographic (relief) information and were often erroneous, since they were only preliminary maps. The topographic and planimetric maps were mostly at a scale of 1:50,000, although a few topographic maps were available at 1:25,000. The government census bureau also produces maps at a scale of 1:50,000 for use by census workers in rural areas. Although these maps were updated every few years with regard to trails and villages, they were often deficient when it came to natural features of the landscape.

Even when we had reliable topographic maps for a particular sector in which we were looking for archaeological sites, there was typically some imprecision in determining the exact location of those sites on the maps. That is because most sites were discovered as we walked on foot over roads and trails that may or may not have been shown accurately on the maps. When we discovered a site on or near a road or trail, we still had to determine where we were, and this usually involved triangulation using a compass. I would stand at what appeared to be the middle of the site and take compass readings to two or more landmarks, which usually were mountain peaks but also might be a distant church steeple or some other human-made structure. In some cases, there was no visible landmark, either natural or artificial, because we were too far from such things or because of low clouds or tall trees. In those instances, we had to estimate how far we had walked. In other situations, if a site was discovered relatively near a road, we used the vehicle odometer to give us the distance (to within tenths of kilometers) from a landmark along the road, such as a bridge or kilometer marker. Even this technique failed us when the odometer on the vehicle stopped working for a few weeks.

All in all, we did the best we could in describing how to reach the site and where it was located to make it feasible for us or other researchers to revisit the same site in the future. There can be no guarantee, however, that all the site coordinates are exact.

By the short 1996 season, we were able to take advantage of the relatively new GPS (global positioning system) technology to determine the site coordinates with greater accuracy. The GPS system, developed and maintained by the U.S. Department of Defense, uses a handheld device that receives signals from satellites in earth orbit. The signal from each satellite allows the GPS receiver to calculate the coordinates and elevation of the site. Prior to the year 2000, the U.S. Defense Department, in order to maintain a military advantage, intentionally reduced the accuracy of the system for civilian use so that a site location could usually be determined only to within about 100 meters. As of 2000, that built-in inaccuracy for civilian receivers was removed, so site coordinates in the future should be accurate to within a few meters or less. Because this new technology was not available during most of the survey project and because there has not yet been time to revisit all of the approximately 300 sites, many of the site locations are still only approximations. Also, GPS does not work in canyons, some valleys, or areas of dense forest where the receiver is unable to obtain clear satellite signals. Nonetheless, in 1996 we found that for previously recorded sites where we used GPS to check the coordinates, our earlier estimates were usually very close to the ones obtained through GPS.

THE SURVEY STRATEGY

The strategy guiding any research project has to be predicated on the goals of the research. Given that nearly all of Western Pichincha was unexplored archaeologically prior to this project, the goals were quite general and broad:

- Salvage part of the North Andean archaeological record by investigating a region of rapid development and concomitant site destruction
- Perform a regional survey in the northern Andes of South America in order to focus on broad cultural development over time and space
- Survey the western flank of the Andes from the summit of the Andes to the Pacific coastal plain to study cultural and developmental similarities and differences with the coast and sierra

Under these broad objectives, more specific goals were laid out prior to the start of the project:

- Determine the antiquity of human occupation of the region
- Identify early agricultural/pottery-making complexes (Formative cultures) that connect the northern sierra Cotocollao culture with well-known Formative coastal cultures, including Valdivia, Machalilla, and Chorrera (all of which were the focus of my previous research)
- Determine the nature of early human adaptation to the different types of rainforest in the region
- Define the various pottery complexes of the region and establish a tentative ceramic chronology for dating sites
- Define distinct prehistoric cultures of the region and determine their spheres of influence
- Catalog extant pre-Columbian structures, including tolas (artificial earthen mounds), house foundations, and forts
- Trace the evolution of trade within the region and with the coast and highlands, and search for trade routes
- Determine the degree of Inca incursion and supremacy in the region

Given these multifarious objectives, the enormous size of the research region, a very limited budget, and the special challenges of accessibility, visibility, and cartography, a regional survey at first glance appears impractical. The standard survey techniques of systematic field walking and shovel testing to locate sites and collect artifacts were unquestionably not feasible. In fact, I spent the first two months of fieldwork in 1984 traveling around Western Pichincha, becoming more familiar with the region and desperately trying to think of new ways to approach a survey in an area where the classic methods were inoperable. By the end of two months, I had a fair idea of specific techniques to use, although our survey methods continued to evolve during the first couple of years.

To give the reader who is unfamiliar with classic archaeological surveying a sense of what should have been done but could not be done, I present Figure 4.2. This map shows the entire research region covered by a grid. Within each major ecological zone, a percentage, say 10%, of randomly selected grid units is marked for systematic surveying. Within each selected grid, the survey team is expected to perform a complete pedestrian survey, visually inspecting the entire surface area and marking and retrieving surface artifacts. In areas with vegetative cover, small test holes dug with a shovel at regular intervals (the shovel-testing method) provide a sampling of what lies near the surface. This strategy is known as a stratified random quadrat sample and is considered one of several desirable strategies that will provide data susceptible to statistical manipulation to represent the entire research region. It is called "stratified" because each environmental zone is sampled independently, "random" because each surveyed grid within each environmental zone is selected using a table of random numbers rather than intuitively, and "quadrat" since the basic survey unit is a quadrat or square. None of this could actually be done for the reasons already noted.

Figure 4.3, on the other hand, is a map of the region showing the land area that was actually surveyed during the various field seasons from 1984 to 1997. Obviously, the survey performed bears no resemblance to the ideal survey. What was actually done I have chosen to refer to as an *opportunistic survey* rather than a sys-

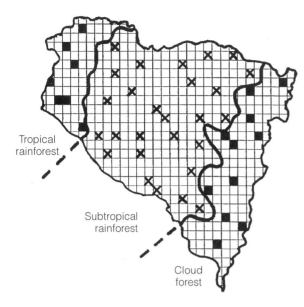

Tropical rainforest

Subtropical rainforest

Cloud forest

Figure 4.2 The Western Pichincha research region with superimposed grid showing areas that might have been surveyed intensively given a systematic stratified quadrat strategy

tematic one. An opportunistic survey includes those improvised methods and techniques that provide for surface inspection of any sectors that have been opened up through natural or human disturbance. Whereas a systematic sample is performed so as to provide optimal representative coverage of a region, an opportunistic sample is performed to provide whatever coverage is possible.

The specific methods used in combination that resulted in the opportunistic sample of Figure 4.3 are presented in the following text.

Inspection of Roads

Pedestrian surveys along roads turned out to be the most utilized method of the project. Bulldozers move a considerable amount of soil in creating roads, and often expose archaeological sites in the process. Road building is also accompanied by removal of vegetation within the right-of-way, which facilitates surveying. Artifacts may be visible in road cuts (where the machinery has cut through a hill) as well as in the roadbed. Some roads were covered with gravel or crushed stone brought in from quarries, and those roadbeds were not surveyed due to the possibility of "contamination" (finding artifacts trucked in from a distance). Needless to say, any artifacts found in the dirt roadbeds were generally very fractured due to foot, horse, or vehicular traffic. It is also safe to assume that they were in a secondary context, presumably near to but not in exactly the same position in which they were originally discarded.

Inspection of Footpaths

Various kinds of trails for horses and pedestrians are much more common than vehicular roads, but they are less likely to reveal archaeological sites because they are so narrow and usually do not erode significantly into the surface. Nonetheless, because trails were so common and provided access to many sectors not having roads, this method was frequently used. As will be discussed in Chapter 7, some trails that were quite deeply eroded turned out to be ancient paths.

Figure 4.3 The Western Pichincha research region showing transects actually surveyed on foot using an opportunistic strategy

Inspection of Sites Identified by Local Inhabitants

Whenever residents of the region informed us of possible archaeological sites based on their observations over the years, we made every effort to visit those sites and to authenticate the purported remains. More often than not, these well-intentioned reports turned out to be bogus; as is true in many parts of the world, even well-educated persons with no archaeological experience often mistakenly identify natural objects as artifacts or natural hills as artificial mounds. Reports of mounds almost always turned out to be spurious, in part because many rural Ecuadorians understand the word *tola* slightly differently from the way archaeologists use it, and in part because mounds are often difficult to distinguish from natural features. Even archaeologists working in Ecuador sometimes confuse hills and artificial mounds through only casual observation. Trying to authenticate such information usually led us on a wild-goose chase, but occasionally these reported sites turned out to be valid and worth our trouble.

Using Place Names to Locate Sites

Certain local place names appearing on maps often indicated the presence of a site. For example, Inca forts were typically built on hilltops and consisted of stone walls arranged in concentric ovals. To a casual observer, these ruins may appear from above like a spiral, and they are often called *churos* (snails) on maps because of their shape. The word *tola* frequently occurs on maps; sometimes the name actually marks the location of mounds and sometimes not, perhaps because the mounds have disappeared over time or because someone once mistook a natural elevation for a mound. We were also interested in locating an ancient salt mine or salt spring reported by the Spanish, so we were always suspicious of the Quichua word *cachi* (salt) or *cachiyacu* (salt water) on maps. Even the words *Yumbo* and *Inga* (Inca) appeared in a few places throughout Western Pichincha, leading us to those locations to look for ruins or other evidence of Yumbo or Inca presence.

Systematic Surveying of Cleared Fields

Fields recently cleared of vegetation either for construction or for planting were few, small, and far between, but we always took advantage of such fields when we came across them. Whenever they were encountered, we would systematically walk the clearing and collect artifacts from the exposed surface. It is significant that practically any time we found such a clearing, there was an archaeological site there, suggesting that the prehistoric occupation of Western Pichincha was very widespread. Unfortunately (from an archaeological perspective), such clearings were all too rare.

Searches Based on Ethnohistoric Records

The Spanish colonial record summarized briefly in the previous chapter also provided a basis for surveying. In particular, Yumbo or Nigua villages, even though they are nonexistent today, are referred to, and enough geographic information is included in archival data to suggest their approximate locations. Concerted efforts were made to survey these localities in order to identify the "lost towns." This method was sometimes successful, sometimes not. It was complicated by the aforementioned fact that Indian "towns" in the region were dispersed rather than nucleated; they were not really villages so much as loose clusters of scattered houses.

These various methods used in combination resulted in the survey pattern illustrated in Figure 4.3. While the survey was not systematic in the usual sense of the word, every effort was made to do opportunistic surveys throughout the region, leaving no major sectors completely unexplored. In that sense, the survey was successful. As will be seen in Chapters 7–8, the amount of information obtained from this haphazard survey was very substantial.

GETTING PERMISSION

Although an agency of the Ecuadorian government gave us permission to conduct archaeological research in the region, we were responsible, as is usually the case, for getting permission from individual landowners to enter their property. In most cases, however, we crossed private property without being able to detect property lines (fences are not widely used except where cattle have been introduced) and carried out our daily surveys without encountering any owners or caretakers of whom we might ask permission. After all, we were surveying in many areas that are considered wilderness, even though some lands within those areas have been legally purchased or homesteaded or have been claimed by squatters' rights. When we did encounter local inhabitants, we usually took a few minutes to engage them in conversation, explain our work, ask for permission to walk over their property, and inquire about any sites they might know. During the many seasons of fieldwork, we found the people (whether homesteaders, poor squatters, or wealthy absentee landowners), almost without exception, to be very friendly and cooperative. Rarely were we turned away, and then it was usually by a family that was employed as caretakers for a wealthy landowner who lived in a distant city rather than on his or her land; in these cases, the caretakers usually instructed us to contact the landowner in Quito or elsewhere to get permission.

CATALOGING SITES

One of the most fundamental concepts in archaeology is that of the *site,* which is defined as a cluster of artifacts, features, and/or ecofacts[1] that indicate human presence in antiquity. While the concept may seem simple, in the field it can become complicated even during a systematic survey, and downright tricky in a survey such as the one we were performing. Archaeologists do not agree on the minimum density of artifacts for defining a site. The simplest conceivable site might be a single small stone flake in isolation, while the most complex is an ancient city. Finding just one flake in isolation does not tell the archaeologist very much and really reduces the concept of site down to something that may not be at all useful in understanding the past.

The techniques used for finding sites in this densely forested region often revealed only a very small part of what may have been a large site. Perhaps the trail cut through only a corner of a site, thereby explaining why there were so few artifacts. On the other hand, a very small site may have been used by only a few people for a few hours, and the little material found on the surface might be representative of what lies below. In some instances, we followed a road or path for a kilometer or more and found a very low density of artifacts distributed nearly continuously along the trail. Does that distribution signal a very large town, a series of somewhat dispersed farmsteads, or several very small and separate sites that were occupied at different times but which now seem to overlap?

These and similar complexities continually plagued us as we proceeded with the survey. As our procedure evolved over the course of the project, we did not always define sites by the same criteria. Nonetheless, since our objective was not simply to find out how many different sites there were in the region but rather to see how humans utilized space over time, what was most important was simply recording artifacts and features where they were found and then going back and trying to make sense of the distribution.

The only artifacts ever found during the many field seasons were potsherds, and occasionally other ceramic pieces, small stone tools or unused flakes, and ground stone tools. If only one or a few tiny artifacts were found over an area, we began to treat that as an isolated find (as opposed to a "site"), but we cataloged the finds just as we would have cataloged a larger number of artifacts or features such as mounds

---

[1]Ecofacts are a category of archaeological data consisting of unmodified materials that were taken to the site by its former occupants or that occur there naturally and help specialists in reconstructing the ancient environment or human activity. Examples are animal bones, fish scales, fossil pollen, and charred plant remains.

or stone walls. The only difference is that we expected to learn something useful about the indigenous peoples from sites, whereas isolated finds held little promise. Altogether, we cataloged nearly 300 sites and a couple dozen isolated finds. This does not mean that we discovered some 300 discrete occupations or locales for human activities; what it means is that we identified approximately 300 locations where humans were present in antiquity and left some evidence that we could find on the modern surface.

Upon discovering a site or isolated find, we had to take adequate notes so that detailed site registry forms could be filled out back in Quito. Enough time was spent at each site to describe as precisely as possible the location of the site and directions on how to arrive at it, as well as the apparent size and density of the site (if this could be determined with any confidence). We also described the natural environment, including relief, vegetation, nearby water sources, soil conditions, and the current condition of the site (e.g., banana plantation, disturbed by road cut, severely eroded, disturbed by looters, etc.). Artifacts visible on the surface of the site were collected and labeled for laboratory analysis. If there were few artifacts, as was often the case, we collected whatever we could find. At sites with a dense accumulation of artifacts visible on the ground surface, we began by collecting everything in small areas of the site and then continued by collecting only those artifacts, especially diagnostic potsherds and stone tools, that would be most useful in determining the age and cultural affiliation of the site. If there were any visible structures at the site, such as mounds or walls, they were sketched and photographed. In fact, photographs were taken of nearly every site to augment the written notes. The Archaeology Museum of the Central Bank, for whom we worked during the early years of the project, had its own forms for recording site data, and we used those forms for cataloging all new discoveries.

The National Institute of Cultural Heritage (INPC in Spanish) is the Ecuadorian government agency that oversees archaeological research and grants permits for work such as ours. That agency also maintains a registry of all known archaeological sites in the country. Upon filling out the site forms, we made copies and submitted them to the INPC for filing and reference by other archaeologists.

Sites were coded in three different ways, according to common practice and the requirements of the INPC. Ecuador uses the same system found in most countries of the Americas, in which sites are identified according to local political units. In the United States, this means sites are identified by state, then county, then by a number indicating their order of discovery. For example, the prehistoric city of Cahokia near Collinsville, Illinois, has a site code of 11-Ms-2, where "11" stands for Illinois, "Ms" for Madison County, and "2" for the second archaeological site cataloged in that county. In Ecuador, this system has been adapted to designate the province, the canton, the parish, and the order of discovery. Accordingly, the site P-LB-Mi-7 is the Nambillo site (discussed in Chapters 5–6), which was the seventh site registered in Mindo parish (Mi) of Los Bancos canton (LB) of Pichincha province (P). For the sake of simplicity, I will identify sites in this book at times simply by their parish and number (e.g., Mi-7) instead of writing out the entire designation. Because the central government occasionally creates or realigns cantons and parishes, some sites had to be recodified to reflect changing political boundaries.

The INPC also requires that sites be identified by coordinates, and there are two widely used global coordinate systems. The first is the familiar latitude and longitude system that measures degrees, minutes, and seconds north or south of the equator and east or west of the prime meridian. Because this system uses base 60 and is not readily convertible into common English or metric units, we also use another coordinate system known as UTM (Universal Transverse of Mercator). This numerical system is metric, so the coordinates are directly convertible into meters or kilometers on maps that have a printed kilometer grid on them.

In order to protect unguarded archaeological sites from depredation by looters or tourists, the catalog information, including coordinates, is available only to professional archaeologists.

THE SUBSURFACE TESTING OF THE NAMBILLO SITE

Although an enormous amount of information can be obtained through regional surveys, we projected from the beginning of the project the need to do some subsurface testing at one or a few sites fairly early in the project in order to provide supplemental data. The two most important reasons for augmenting the survey data with excavation data are the following. First, the survey stage of the project was expected to lead eventually to an excavation stage, and it was uncertain how feasible it would be to excavate and find substantial physical remains in this tropical rainforest habitat. The dense vegetation, logistical challenges, acidic soil, and very high humidity all conspire to make excavations difficult and to degrade the physical remains. Doing a test excavation fairly early would help to determine whether an excavation stage of the project would likely be worth the trouble. Our work at the Nambillo site showed us that excavation projects in the region were indeed feasible, that the site was in reasonably good condition despite millennia of volcanic activity and forest growth, and that subsistence data (especially animal bones and charred seeds) were going to be hard to come by in that environment.

Secondly, a significant drawback to survey data based on the collection and study of surface artifacts is that stratigraphic information is excluded. Even though it is possible to establish a chronological sequence for artifacts based on changing styles in surface collections (a method known as "seriation"), it is exceedingly difficult to do unless pottery is abundant and fairly elaborately decorated, which was clearly not going to be the case for most of Western Pichincha. Even when a seriation can be performed, distinguishing between the start and the finish is still dependent on the kind of external data most likely to come from stratigraphic excavations. Only by observing the sequence of pottery styles (or whatever other category of artifacts is being used) in the ground from bottom to top can one be certain that the ordering of artifacts is reliable. By performing limited test excavations at one or a few sites early on, we would then have a sort of anchor upon which to build and refine our ceramic chronology. As it turned out, the excavations at Nambillo provided sufficient pottery in a clear stratigraphic sequence to create a timeline that can be used, at least tentatively, for much of Western Pichincha and that can be related to pottery sequences in neighboring areas. These results and others will be discussed more fully in the next two chapters.

5/How to "X-ray" a Deeply Buried Cloud Forest Site

THE NAMBILLO SITE AND ITS SETTING

The Nambillo site (P-LB-Mi-7) in Mindo parish was discovered fairly early during our surveys and immediately was considered a site that might merit excavation. This is because a road was cut through the site and revealed at least three different superimposed series of occupations going back as far as the Formative Period, and these occupation strata were very nicely separated from each other by intervening volcanic sediments. Only one other site found during surveying was clearly comparable in terms of its long duration and clear stratigraphy, but additional work at that other site was not feasible due to a washed-out road that made access too difficult.

Mindo (Figure 5.1) is located approximately in the center of Yumbo territory and within view—when the clouds dissipate temporarily—both of the Andean peaks and the foot of the Andes. The small, picturesque town of Mindo lies in a beautiful valley drained by a river of the same name. The valley is surrounded by very steep-sided mountains that are covered with dense cloud forest vegetation. Jutting into the valley is a ridge of mountains called the San Lorenzo Cordillera that runs down from Pichincha volcano and ends very near the town of Mindo. This descending ridge is bounded on one side by the Mindo River and on the other by the Nambillo River. The ridge is narrow and very steep-sided. While the valley floor lies at about 1,200 m (3,960 ft.) above sea level, the Nambillo site starts at 1,500 m (4,950 ft.) and continues upward along the ascending ridge to about 1,600 m (5,280 ft.).

Just a couple of years before we first surveyed around Mindo, a local inhabitant opened a narrow dirt road that ran several kilometers up the ridge from the town. This was done in order to allow him and others in the vicinity easier access to the timber and potential pastureland along the narrow ridge. Several archaeological sites along the ridge top were exposed by the bulldozing activity during road construction. In fact, as we walked the road, we found bits of pottery and stone flakes over the entire 10-km (6-mi.) length. Based on changes in artifact densities, we hypothesized that this was not one extremely large site but rather a series of small occupations (possibly individual farmsteads for the most part) that overlapped over time. The ridge was unoccupied in modern times, though a couple of huts in the vicinity were

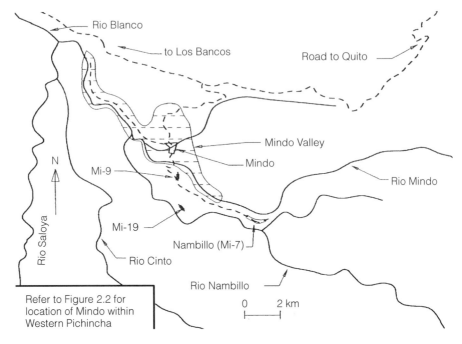

Figure 5.1 The Mindo area of Western Pichincha

occasionally used by Mindo residents for a few days at a time while working their lands.

Lower down the ridge toward Mindo, we discovered two larger sites with earthen mounds. The first of these (site Mi-9) consisted of one very large rectangular platform mound, and the other (Mi-19), a short distance farther up the ridge, comprised four smaller platform mounds. The Nambillo site lay some 4 km farther up the ridge but seemed more promising to us than the tola sites because of its many superimposed occupations. Our primary objective in excavating a site in the midst of a survey project was to get stratigraphic information from a deep, multicomponent (that is, having more than one period of occupation) site. Nambillo seemed a very good bet and indeed turned out to be valuable in providing a base chronology for the area.

Because the San Lorenzo Cordillera is so narrow and steep, the only practical way to traverse it is to follow the crest. This is where the road was built and our survey was necessarily limited to that roadbed. In a few places, such as at the two tola sites, the ridge widened out and there was space for a slightly more sprawling settlement. In other areas, especially at the Nambillo site, the ridge consisted of a sequence of small hills one after another. These hillocks provided slightly more ample living space and were separated by quite narrow areas where the ridge dropped off very abruptly both to the left and right. One could imagine a drunk man walking along this section of the ridge and staggering to one side or the other. Whichever way he went, within a few feet he would begin tumbling a few hundred meters down toward the river, his fall being broken only by the dense vegetation. Such was the narrowness and steepness of the ridge in places.

Although it was not possible to determine the exact boundaries of the various sites along the ridge because of the more or less continuous distribution of artifacts, what we defined as the Nambillo site ran for about 1.9 km (1.2 mi.). The only potential living spaces, then, were at these small hills and these were labeled by letters to represent the major sectors of the Nambillo site. The first hillock was A, the second B, and so on to H. Figure 5.2 is a simplified map that gives an overview of the site and shows the eight hills that represent the eight primary activity loci within the site.

SOME BACKGROUND ON MINDO

The town of Mindo was listed by Spanish chroniclers as an ancient Yumbo settlement, and there are a few references to missionary work and road-building activities that took place during the Spanish colonial period. The missionary work was mostly unsuccessful, as the native inhabitants complained repeatedly about abuses by the priest and their population dwindled considerably due to forced migrations for road building, high mortality due to Spanish-introduced disease, and probably to migration deeper into the forest from the Mindo Valley to avoid exploitation. By the late 1800s, the ancient settlement of Mindo had reportedly disappeared.

Beginning around 1906, a mestizo settler from the sierra purchased most of the then uninhabited (or nearly so) Mindo Valley and began opening it up for recolonization. He donated land in the valley for a new town, and the population gradually grew through the 20th century to approximately 2,000 people by 1990. The sleepy little town isolated by the lack of a good road remained mostly cut off from both the highlands and coast until a new highway opened within a few miles of Mindo in 1995. The establishment of a very large cloud forest preserve nearby and the construction of various ecotourism facilities has recently transformed this once forgotten village into a small but vibrant destination for international ecotourism. The Nambillo site, which used to be readily accessible in a sort of no-man's land, has been fenced off by a private owner for a hiking trail open to paying tourists only, though the cloud forest vegetation is still intact and the presence of the archaeological site is not generally known.

The people who settled in Mindo in the 1900s were mostly mestizos from various parts of Ecuador and even Colombia as well as coastal inhabitants of African descent from Esmeraldas province to the northwest of Pichincha. Both my crew and a team of ethnographers I put together looked high and low for vestiges of Yumbo culture in the modern settlement of Mindo, but that search was almost entirely unsuccessful. A very few families of Mindo are probably descended from pre-1900 settlers of the cloud forest and perhaps even from remnant Yumbo populations. One very elderly woman in Mindo was reputed to be the granddaughter of the last Yumbo "chief" of Mindo, but she was of such advanced age when we interviewed her that she was not able to confirm that descent or provide us with any information about the ancient populations there. Modern Mindo has very little or no cultural continuity with the ancient Yumbo settlement of Mindo.

Nonetheless, the small town (before it became a tourist destination) served as our home for approximately six months from late 1985 to early 1986. We rented a house in the town and set it up as our living quarters and laboratory. We drove approximately 40 minutes each way to and from the Nambillo site high up the ridge.[1] Living

---

[1]That means it took us about 40 minutes to travel roughly 8 km by jeep, which gives an average speed of 12 km/hr (19 mi/hr). That should give the reader some idea how poor the road was.

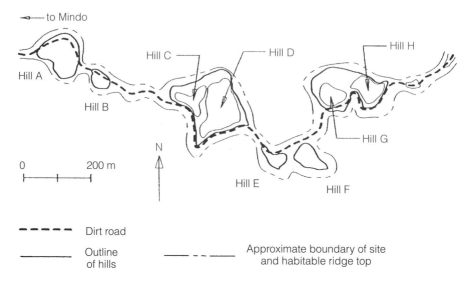

Figure 5.2 Simplified relief map of Nambillo site showing the eight hills

in this small town solved various logistical problems; it certainly would have been much too difficult to sustain a field camp nearer the Nambillo site given the lack of shelter and food, and the arduous climbing one had to do to get fresh water. While climbing very steep, heavily forested mountains each day to get water is routine for the modern montaña folks and presumably was not a problem for the Yumbos, it is especially strenuous for those of us accustomed to a much less tiring existence at lower elevation and in flatter country and to spending several hours a day in an office.

SOIL CORING AT NAMBILLO[2]

Having performed two separate inspections of the site before making a final decision to conduct an excavation project there, we hired a professional topographer (land surveyor) to make a relief map of Nambillo. Such mapping is often done by the archaeologists themselves, but in this case, with the very rugged mountainous terrain and dense vegetation plus the limited time we had available to set up the project, we decided to enlist the help of a professional. Our project budget was quite modest, but the administrators of the Museum of the Central Bank were willing to allow me to contract a specialist in this particular instance. In some other situations, we simply had to perform analyses ourselves or hold off on them due to the absence of funds.

The normal method archaeologists prefer to use to begin an intensive study of an archaeological site once it is mapped is that of a systematic surface collection. This allows the researchers to define more confidently the boundaries of the site as well as to identify areas of more and less artifact concentration. Even the types of artifacts or structures found on the surface are useful in planning an excavation project. However, as was true with the general survey of all of Western Pichincha, traditional methods were not feasible; once again we had to improvise.

---

[2]An earlier and somewhat more technical version of this section and the following three sections was published in the *Journal of Field Archaeology;* see Lippi (1988) in the References.

The dirt road that bisected the long, narrow site of Nambillo cut a very narrow transect only some 3–5 m (10–16 ft.) wide. While this provided an invaluable peek at what lay beneath the surface, it did not give us enough information upon which to plan an efficient excavation strategy. No artifacts were visible on the ground surface due to the very dense jungle vegetation and the layers of tephra (volcanic ash, sand, and pumice). We could simply have elected to place test excavations randomly over the eight hillocks, a strategy that would have been *very* inefficient, or try to find a way to understand what lay beneath our feet prior to excavating. Borrowing from another discipline, I hit upon a minimally destructive way to study the buried soils. Pedology (soil science), a subfield of geology, uses two methods appropriate to our objectives. Those methods are stratigraphic studies by way of soil coring and the identification of areas of human activity by phosphate analysis.

Soil coring is certainly not new to archaeology, since archaeologists occasionally make use of soil cores to probe quickly into underlying strata. However, the use of soil cores by archaeologists is typically unsystematic; that is, a core is taken when and where it seems useful, but usually there is no attempt to perform a methodical sampling. We decided to begin our subsurface investigation of the site with a very careful and systematic coring of selected hills.

Soil corers are of different types, but the most useful for inspecting the soil strata consists of a steel cylinder with a sharp cutting edge welded to a long steel pole with a T-bar handle at the top. We knew that the site with its various buried horizons (soil strata lying underneath volcanic sediments) was as much as 3–4 m (10–13 ft.) deep, and some of the layers were very dense clay that is hard to cut through. We could not afford an elaborate hydraulic corer, but with the aid of geologists at a soil laboratory at a university in Quito, we had a machinist build a special coring tool for us with a sample cylinder 8 cm in diameter and with rod extensions that allowed us to probe as much as 4 m deep.

We had another problem, which is that the hillocks of Nambillo were in a cloud forest and covered by extremely dense vegetation. We had to do some clearing in the most efficient manner in order to proceed with the coring. A geographer by the name of Robert Eidt (1984), who had been interested in the same problems, pioneered a strategy for such sampling during work in Colombia. In accordance with his sugges-tion, we did the following: At the top of each hill, we established a datum point (a permanent stake in the ground that served as reference point), and then we took soil cores along lines radiating out from the datum at 30° intervals. Along each radial, we performed a soil core at 5-m intervals. Each core was labeled according to the hill, the radial (where 0° represents north, 90° east, and so forth), and the horizontal dis-tance from the datum point. An example of a coring location is: B-120°-20m. Occasionally it was necessary to vary a little from the 5-m interval if a large tree was in the way.

As a first step, we had to hire a couple of workers from Mindo to cut through the undergrowth with machetes to create clear lines of sight. This clearing of radial lines also allowed us to set up a transit at the datum point and make a more detailed relief map of the modern surface of each hill than the professional topographer had been able to do when he mapped the entire sector. An added advantage to this strategy of radial testing rather than the usual square grid testing is that the clearing of vegeta-tion was minimal, leaving most of the site undisturbed (Figure 5.3).

As fieldwork got underway, I had a crew of two Ecuadorian university students in archaeology (three for a short time) as well as three men from Mindo who helped

Marco Suárez

Figure 5.3 The author uses a transit in a cleared area of Hill D while mapping that section of the site.

with the work as needed, such as clearing vegetation with machetes, something at which we were very clumsy and they were very skilled. As the laborers worked at clearing lines of sight over the various hills, the rest of us began the soil coring operation. At first this proved to be very difficult work because some of the soil horizons were very clayey and difficult to core. We actually broke our specially made coring tool a couple of times before coming to realize that a constant sharpening of the edge was crucial. After repairs to the tool and the purchase of a hand-cranked grinding wheel for the site, the pace of coring picked up. As one person worked the corer vertically into the ground, the other checked for changes in soil color or texture (the size of the grains) and measured the vertical distance to each new stratum (Figure 5.4). Once in a while the core sample contained an artifact, such as a small sherd or a stone flake. These artifacts were bagged and labeled. Eventually, two of the laborers were also trained in identifying the various soil horizons and were able to take over the work as the students and I turned our attention to the stratigraphic excavations.

THE STRATIGRAPHY

The soil probes at Nambillo provided a wealth of information upon which to determine the stratigraphy of the site prior to excavations. What follows is a general stratigraphic description that holds for much of the site, keeping in mind that there was slight variance from this at times. Table 5.1 is a summary of the information provided below.

The uppermost stratum, labeled Stratum I, was simply the humus that forms as the vegetative matter decomposes and begins to mix with inorganic materials, thereby forming a new soil horizon. At Nambillo the humus was typically 5–15 cm

Figure 5.4 Marco Suárez works the coring tool on Hill B while Oswel Bahamonde looks on, ready to take notes. Both were Ecuadorian archaeology students and project assistants.

TABLE 5.1   NAMBILLO STRATIGRAPHY—GENERALIZED FOR THE ENTIRE SITE

Stratum	Description	Typical Thickness	Excavation Levels
I	Humus (decomposing floral and faunal matter on mineral soil surface)	5–15 cm	1 culturally sterile level
II	Tephra (volcanic sand, ash, and pumice)	5–20 cm	1 sterile level
III	Transition between tephra and Paleosol 1	15 cm	1 sterile level; 2nd level with few artifacts
IV	Paleosol 1: buried soil; very dark brown silty clay	35–80 cm	8–9 levels distinguished as separate occupation floors or by more noticeable tephra
V	Tephra	0–40 cm	1 sterile level
VI	Palesol 2: buried soil; dark brown silty clay	10–50 cm	1st level with artifacts; 2nd level very few artifacts
VII	Tephra	100–140 cm	1 very thick sterile level; artifacts begin to appear very near Paleosol 3
VIII	Paleosol 3: buried soil; black clay	25–40 cm	3–5 levels distinguished as separate occupation floors or by more noticeable tephra
IX	Subsoil (inorganic yellowish clay and weathered bedrock)	unknown	culturally sterile
	Total	195–400 cm	

thick and was not found to contain any archaeological materials. Immediately below this was Stratum II, consisting of volcanic tephra. We were quite confident, based on vulcanological studies, that this thin layer of ash, pumice, and sand was the result of the eruption of Pichincha (just a few kilometers to the southeast of Nambillo) in 1660, an eruption that was described in detail by Spanish residents in Quito.

Below this, Stratum III was a mixture of the sand and pumice of Stratum II with the darker clayey soil that lay beneath. In other words, Stratum III was a transitional layer resulting from the natural mixing of components over time. Near the bottom of this stratum, we began to encounter the first few artifacts.

Stratum IV will be referred to here as Paleosol 1. A paleosol (often called a "buried soil") is an organic soil horizon that has been covered over by sediments, such as the volcanic tephra referred to above. Prior to the eruption of Pichincha, this stratum was the ground surface that gradually built up over time, and it contained evidence of a series of human occupations probably spanning several centuries. Each separate occupation is denoted by a horizontal concentration of artifacts and is separated by soil with few or no artifacts.

Below Paleosol 1 is Stratum V, another layer of volcanic sediments, and below this (in Stratum VI) is the second buried soil, Paleosol 2. This pattern continues downward: Stratum VII is a much thicker layer of volcanic tephra, providing evidence of catastrophic volcanic activity that put a temporary end to human habitation of the area. Below this (in Stratum VIII) is the third and final buried soil, Paleosol 3. Immediately below that (in Stratum IX), soil is a thin layer of subsoil formed mainly from the breakdown of the underlying bedrock. This was the lowest stratum and the "bottom" of the site.

By the way, the only stratum that could be directly dated based on historical information was Stratum II, which clearly corresponds to the 1660 eruption of Pichincha. It is not reliable to calculate the age of other strata based on their thickness or depth below the surface, contrary to what many casual observers at archaeological sites may think. For example, the very thick Stratum VII may have accumulated within a single year or perhaps a few years, whereas there is good reason to believe that the relatively thin Stratum VIII (Paleosol 3) may have accumulated over several centuries. In order to date strata that are not clearly related to known historic events, one has to resort to chemical or other dating techniques that require special analyses after the fieldwork is completed. Methods that were useful for Nambillo will be discussed in the following chapter.

Virtually all of the artifacts, with very few exceptions due to mixing, were found within the three paleosols, making it possible to state unequivocally that there were three major occupation periods at the site and that each one was followed by one or more volcanic eruptions. Within each paleosol, there is more or less evidence of horizontal banding of artifacts, suggesting discrete occupations within each major period. This phenomenon is discussed further in Chapter 6.

THE PALEOTOPOGRAPHY

Our ability to distinguish the beginning and ending of the different strata during the soil coring procedure provided us with an unexpected bonanza of data. Since we knew the depth of the top of each of three paleosols over various parts of the site, it occurred to me that we could create relief maps of the different hills representing dif-

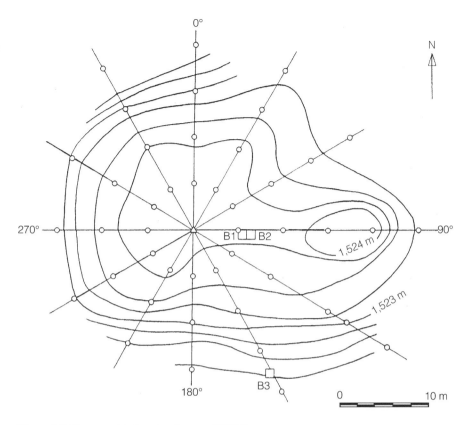

Figure 5.5 Topographic (contour) map of Hill B

ferent times in the past when each paleosol was the exposed soil prior to a volcanic eruption. This would show us how each hill had changed in size and form over time and would also indicate what the immediate landscape looked like during any partic-ular occupation period. I decided to name this method *paleotopography,* a term that means ancient topography and seemed to reasonably describe what we were doing. Much to my surprise, upon returning to the United States a few months after finish-ing these buried surface maps, I read a recent article in a major archaeology journal in which another archaeologist (Stein 1986) had done exactly the same thing for a site in Kentucky, and had even used the same term, *paleotopography.* This coincidence should not be too surprising, since our analyses were logical next steps given our data.

As an example of the mapping procedure, I include here some illustrations from Hill B and its underlying "paleohills." The original topographic map (simplified here) for the modern surface of Hill B is shown in Figure 5.5, and this can be easily compared to the two paleohills corresponding to the surface of Paleosols 1 and 3, respectively (Figures 5.6 and 5.7). Note that Paleohill B1 (representing the top of Paleosol 1) is quite similar in size and form to the modern Hill B. However, Paleohill B3 (corresponding to the top of Paleosol 3) shows a quite different land-scape. Paleohill B3 is a smaller hill shifted to the north, and the southeastern part of Hill B was in fact a ravine or gully during the time that Paleosol 3 was the ground

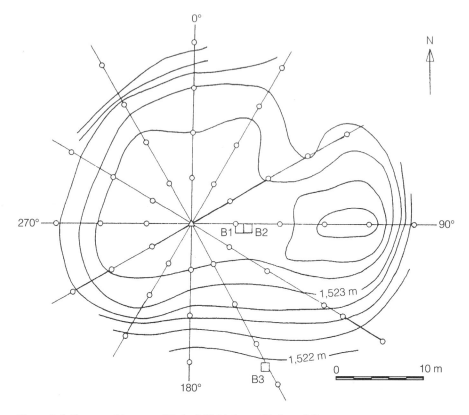

Figure 5.6 Topographic map of Paleohill B1 (top of Paleosol 1)

surface. Because Paleosol 2 was discontinuous and more difficult to identify in the cores, I was not able to map that particular paleohill.

Look for a moment at the three maps again and find the location of the three test excavations labeled B1, B2, and B3. Adjacent cuts B1 and B2 were practically at the top of Hill B and Paleohill B1 and on a fairly level surface, but at the time of Paleosol 3 those cuts were penetrating a hillside, not a level surface. Excavation B3 was on the southeast side of the hill in modern times and during Paleosol 1 occupations, but it was apparently across a gully and on the lower edge of an adjacent hill during the Paleosol 3 occupations.

Another way to look at these "paleomaps" is in cross-section. One such pair of cross-section maps is illustrated in Figure 5.8, in which the upper cross-section is a north-south one while the lower one runs east-west. In this way, it is easy to see how the landform changed over time as volcanic sediments built up over ancient human settlements. This information is useful in reconstructing activities at the site. For example, the area of excavations B1 and B2 may have been a good place to build a house during Paleosol 1 occupations, but a good place to toss garbage during Paleosol 3 occupations.

Another surprising and important discovery in making these paleotopographic maps was the identification of a few archaeological features. Adjacent corings usually had very similar depths to each paleosol, but occasionally one coring would find the paleosol to run much deeper than the surrounding ones. These were interpreted

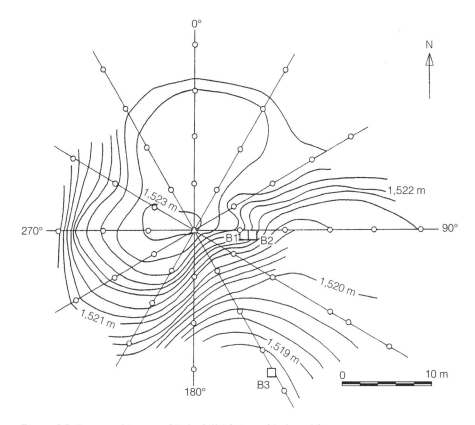

Figure 5.7 Topographic map of Paleohill B3 (top of Paleosol 3)

as human disturbances ("features"), probably the result of the original inhabitants digging holes for garbage, food storage, post erection, and so on. The apparent existence of such domestic features in our sample area further reinforced the notion that we were investigating a habitation site.

PHOSPHATE ANALYSIS OF THE SOILS

Anthrosols are soils that have been structurally or chemically altered by humans. The most significant elements that are added to soil through human activity are nitrogen, phosphorus, and potassium. With the exception of phosphorus, these elements gradually disappear from the soil by leaching, horizontal movement, or gasification. In nature, phosphorus occurs most frequently as inorganic phosphate [$(PO_4)^{3-}$], which reacts with calcium, iron, or aluminum in the soil and becomes practically immovable and insoluble for an indefinite period. Even though phosphorus in this form is not accessible to vegetation, it remains in the soil where it was originally deposited (Eidt 1984:26–27; Limbrey 1975:69–72).

Sources of soil phosphorus are varied (bedrock, fauna, flora, and humans), but the amount deposited by humans is much greater than that from other sources. Here is part of the example that Eidt (1984:30) gave to illustrate this difference: In a pasture of 100 hectares (roughly 2½ acres), one hundred head of cattle increase the

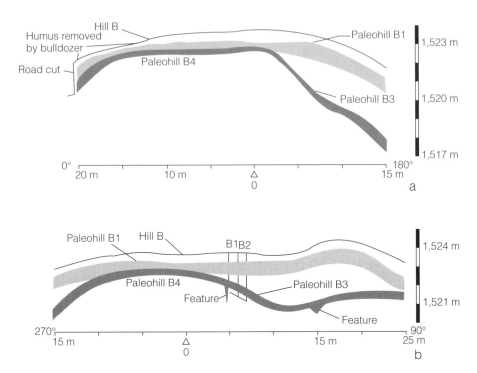

Figure 5.8 Cross-section of Hill B: a. north-south; b. east-west

phosphorus by 4.2 mg/m^2/day, while a settlement of fifty people on 0.1 hectare can be expected to increase phosphorus by 187.6 mg/m^2/day. Most of the phosphorus comes from urine, feces, corpses, food waste, and general organic refuse. Consequently, phosphate analysis of soils can reveal areas where people formerly engaged in household activities, dumped their garbage, or buried their dead.

Archaeologists have known at least since the 1920s that soils taken from archaeological sites can indicate areas of certain kinds of human activity through the accumulation of phosphates, yet the use of phosphate testing has been very restricted over the last 80 years. The first attempt by an archaeologist to use phosphate analysis of soils was not carried out in the United States (or elsewhere in the world to my knowledge) until 1951. After that, the method was used very rarely, in part because archeologists tended to use it where it was not necessary, such as in testing the phosphates of a known burial mound or of household refuse. My first experience with phosphate testing was at the great Cahokia site in Illinois, where our field school director had us collect soils for phosphate analysis from known garbage pits in house floors. The testing merely served to confirm what we already knew. Another problem was that archaeologists tended to measure phosphates using a simple agricultural test that was not particularly precise. Robert Eidt was instrumental in convincing me that the chemical testing had to be done using more than the cheap agricultural kits generally available.

In order to conduct phosphate testing, we collected samples of soil 10 cm below the top of each buried soil horizon during the coring procedure. To protect these samples from contamination by soapy hands or other modern sources of phosphate, we

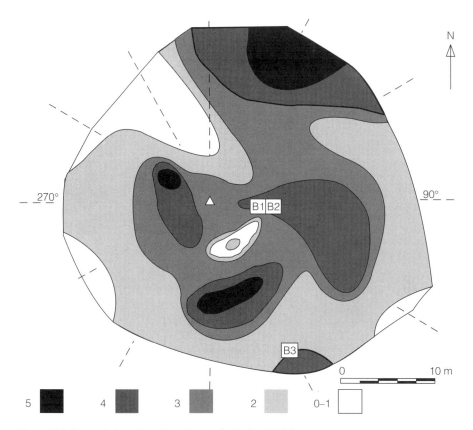

Figure 5.9 Map of phosphate distribution for Paleohill B1

were careful to use a clean trowel and not make hand contact as the samples were bagged and labeled. At first we subjected a small part of each sample to the agricultural phosphate test in our makeshift laboratory in Mindo, but the results were too imprecise to be useful. I then made arrangements for the samples to be taken to the chemistry laboratory of the Museum of the Central Bank in Quito where a chemist performed the phosphate "ring test" as described by Eidt (1984:35–38).[3]

The results of these tests proved to be very useful. Samples for phosphate testing were taken at 10 cm below the top of each of the three paleosols in each core sample. Again, for the sake of illustration, the results from Hill B are illustrated here. Figure 5.9 shows phosphate distribution 10 cm below the top of Paleosol 1, and Figure 5.10 does the same for Paleosol 3. For a significant portion of Figure 5.10, the phosphate reading for Paleosol 3 could not be determined because of possible mixing with Paleosol 2; that part of the map must simply be ignored. What can be seen in that map, though, is that there is not one but rather two areas of phosphate concentration, representing the two different paleohills that underlie Hill B. Even though

---

[3]By the way, Eidt not only improved the fairly simple "ring test" for soil phosphates but also developed a more sophisticated "phosphate fractionation" test, which he claimed could provide much more accurate and useful results. Eidt stated he had evidence from Colombia that not only showed areas of ancient human farming but also suggested, by the "phosphate signature," which crops had been cultivated. Due to budget limitations, we did not get involved in this more complex and controversial testing during the Nambillo season.

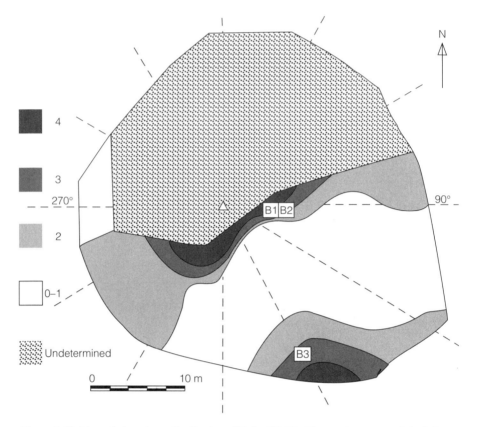

Figure 5.10 Map of phosphate distribution of Paleohill B3. The northern part of the hill was stratigraphically mixed with Paleohill B2, so no measurements were taken.

the area between the two hills was shown to be a gully in Figure 5.7, it becomes clear that it was not used to discard garbage. That particular area seems not to be a good place to conduct excavations. For Figure 5.9, there are a few different concentrations of phosphate, all of which might be worth test excavations. There is also the anomalous white oval of very low phosphates near the center of the hill. It is possible that this small zone was kept clean of any debris or perhaps was used only for inorganic debris, such as might result from flint-knapping, which would not add any phosphate to the soil. The phosphate analysis has not indicated which activities were going on at the site, only where activities were taking place.

All of the work described in this chapter took our very small crew about one month of full-time work and then was followed by additional part-time coring for two more months as part of the crew continued coring and the rest began excavations on hills already cored. The stratigraphic, paleotopographic, and phosphate results, when used together, took much of the guesswork out of determining where to begin the excavation of the site. In effect, we managed to take something analogous to an x-ray of the site, and in doing so caused only a very modest amount of vegetation removal and soil disturbance.

6/Performing
"Exploratory Surgery"
at Nambillo

GETTING STARTED

Excavating is always a very tedious, time-consuming, and, by extension, expensive process. It is never possible to do as much digging as one would want for maximum recovery of data, and it is never advisable, except in instances of salvage, to dig more than one can expect to analyze and interpret in a reasonable time after the field season. Besides the technical skills that are needed, one must also continually make decisions regarding a severely limited budget, time constraints, available staff, and logistics (transportation, lodging, supplies, etc.) All of these concerns make the excavation field season a very intense and stressful period. Nonetheless, you will rarely see an archaeologist in a better mood than when she or he is working at a dig (or in the local tavern or *cantina* often frequented in the evenings). In this chapter, I will discuss the methods and techniques we used at the Nambillo site and some of the results.

It is not at all uncommon in archaeology for the excavation of a site to begin with the solemn but completely arbitrary pronouncement by the project leader, "This spot looks as good as any." Thanks to the coring strategy outlined in the previous chapter, we were able to do better than that. Nonetheless, there are still a lot of unknowns when beginning a dig, and we were further challenged by having a large buried site, a very small crew, and only a few months before the rainy season would begin.[1] It was obvious from the beginning, and completely appropriate given that the Western Pichincha Project was still primarily in survey mode, that any excavating done at Nambillo would be very limited in extent and exploratory in nature.

As has been stated before, we had two primary reasons for taking time out from surveying to conduct some excavations: First, we wanted to obtain a long chronological sequence that could serve as a general timeline for the region (allowing for some variation around the region); we wanted to have clear stratigraphic evidence for the length of habitation and gradual developments by finding pottery, stone tools, and so forth. Secondly, we wanted to test the feasibility of conducting excavations in a

---

[1]It also often rains during the "dry" season, but then at least much of the day is fair, and the rains do not flood the site, as can happen from about January to May.

cloud forest environment. In general, tropical forest archaeology around the world has a bad rap due to the difficult working conditions and the generally poor preservation of archaeological materials. Plant remains and even human and animal bones are often disintegrated by acidic tropical soils, and even the pottery of some tropical forest sites has been in the worst possible condition and barely recognizable. We needed to know whether plans for future extensive excavations were likely to bear fruit or not.

EXCAVATION METHODS AND TECHNIQUES

Given the first objective, it was essential to perform what archaeologists usually call vertical excavations—test pits or trenches scattered across a site that open little surface area but head straight down to the bottom of the site. If we had opted for horizontal or area excavations, we could have spent the entire season excavating a presumed household area in perhaps one or two of the top layers of Paleosol 1, but there would have been no time to explore what lay farther below or to check on other parts of the site.

Based on the results of the coring, we decided to put two or three test pits on as many of the eight hills as time would allow before torrential rains brought the season to a close. As it turned out, we were only able to excavate a total of six test pits on three of the eight hills. By "test pit" (or "excavation unit"), I mean a square, vertical hole that measures one meter by one meter (approximately 3 ft. × 3 ft.). A disadvantage of such narrow excavations is that important features related to the domestic activities—postmolds showing the outline of a house, storage or garbage pits, burials, flint-knapping areas, and so on—are likely to be missed or at least not to be evident. The purpose of digging perfectly square units with absolutely vertical walls is so that the provenience (the exact position within the site) of any artifacts, features, or ecofacts can be precisely measured with respect to the walls of the pit; square units provide for easier record keeping and allow for a systematic expansion of the digging as time allows and objectives require.

"Test pit" often refers to initial 1 m × 1 m cuts made in arbitrary levels in order to determine site stratigraphy. In the case of Nambillo, we already knew the stratigraphy quite well, so we were able to excavate all the pits according to the natural strata. Because arbitrarily excavated cuts often mix materials from different periods, they have little diagnostic value except to indicate how to excavate stratigraphically thereafter. Stratigraphic cuts, on the other hand, keep materials from different strata separate, allowing the analysis and reconstruction of separate occupation episodes. It is well known that even careful stratigraphic excavating does not eliminate all mixing, since artifacts move around in the soil over time due to natural disturbances and sometimes the stratum itself may be slightly disturbed, but the existence of the various thick volcanic tephra sediments virtually precluded any chance of mixing among the three paleosols. We only had to be wary of possible mixing within paleosols.

The test pits on each hill were labeled after the letter of the hill and then sequentially. Hence, A2 was the second test pit on Hill A, and D1 was the first pit on Hill D. The primary excavation tool was the 5-in. pointed masonry trowel, the basic digging tool of most excavation projects. After marking off the 1 m × 1 m grid square (using the same datum point for each hill that was established for the soil coring) and removing the surface vegetation, the excavator used the trowel to scrape the soil very gradually and evenly while watching carefully for artifacts, features, or indications of a stratum boundary. All the soil excavated was passed through a ⅛-in. mesh screen[2] to recover very small artifacts, except for soil samples of a few liters that were collected for flotation (a plant and small bone recovery method described later) or pollen analysis. An excavation level would end when any of three criteria was met: (1) a stratum boundary was reached; (2) an occupation floor was identified; or (3) the level was 10 cm (approx. 4 in.) deep and neither of the other two criteria had been met. That is, the stratum was subdivided arbitrarily into 10 cm thick levels. For protection against the rain that often fell in the afternoon even during the dry season, a plastic tarp was erected over each excavation (Figure 6.1).

By "occupation floor" in the second criterion above, I mean that the excavator found a concentration of artifacts at a particular depth and lying flat (as opposed to being found in random positions from lying flat to standing on end), which could imply that the floor of an ancient house or the ancient ground surface near a house had been reached. It is hypothesized that such artifacts may well be in primary context; that is, they appear to be exactly as they were originally deposited centuries ago. On the other hand, artifacts having different orientations (some flat, some cocked, some on end), found at slightly different depths rather than in a more or less horizontal plane, may be in secondary context, perhaps because they were originally discarded elsewhere and then picked up and dumped where we find them, or perhaps because of the natural mixing that takes place within the soil over time. Either way, we felt it was reasonable to consider the so-called occupation floors as being nearly undisturbed and representing discrete time units, unlike the other artifacts that appeared between such floors.

Very extensive record keeping must be done while excavating. Much to the vexation of many new archaeology students in their first field experience, more time is usually spent taking notes, making maps and drawings, photographing, and collecting and bagging samples than is actually spent digging. In order to ensure that record keeping is systematic and thorough, a series of forms was prepared ahead of time. These had to be filled out for each excavation level, feature, unusual artifact, small piece of charcoal, and so on. Just the basic form for one level in one test pit was two pages long and required a host of measurements, observations, and illustrations. Often, additional pages as well as maps and drawings were attached to this level form.

There are two principal ways to record provenience (the precise location within the site) of artifacts during excavation. One is grid-plotting, and the other is piece-plotting. In the former method, artifacts are labeled according to the excavation unit and level from which they were excavated, so many neighboring artifacts may share the same provenience designation. Piece-plotting is more time-consuming, since the exact location of every cultural object found is measured. For the most part, we conducted grid-plotting in each of the levels within each stratum. However, for special objects, such as unusual artifacts, features, or charcoal samples, we used the piece-plotting method.

We were always careful to keep the walls of the pit as vertical as possible, since those four outer walls served as references for measuring objects within each unit.

---

[2] ¼-in. mesh is more commonly used in archaeology. ⅛-in. mesh works only in soils with low clay content. If there is too much clay, it will not pass through the screen.

Figure 6.1 Marco Suárez takes notes under a plastic tarp while excavating unit D1

For grid-plotting, we carefully measured the exact depth of the level both before and after excavating it. This involved measuring the depth of each corner and of the middle. Since we were following the natural stratigraphy, the levels were sometimes slightly sloped rather than horizontal, and careful measurement of those five points helped to maintain accurate provenience records. Initially, each of the five points was measured by dropping a plumb bob from the four corners and center at ground surface and then using a tape measure to determine the depth below surface. In order to double-check these important measurements, we also used the surveyor's transit and stadia rod (the large "measuring stick" used in land surveying) to check our initial measurements. In those instances when we piece-plotted an object, we used tape measures and a plumb bob to ascertain depths, and we placed a 1 m × 1 m aluminum frame over the floor of the unit to measure horizontal distances. The metal frame had a grid of cords at 10-cm intervals so that piece-plotting could be done accurately and quickly (Figure 6.2). This work was then checked using the transit and stadia rod.

All the excavating was done by two (occasionally three) Ecuadorian university students and myself; I spent at least half my time supervising their work to make sure it was being done as carefully as possible. In addition, we maintained a crew of three laborers from Mindo who were trained in screening soil and sorting and bagging artifacts (as well as protecting us from snakes and tarantulas).

Occasionally, there was a need for smaller tools such as dental picks, small brushes, or tweezers to handle particularly fragile or poorly preserved items. The only use of shovels was during the excavation of Stratum VII, the very thick tephra deposits. Even then, all the sediments were screened for artifacts, and we resorted to using trowels and excavating more carefully as we approached Paleosol 3.

Figure 6.2 Oswel Bahamonde uses the aluminum-and-string mapping grid to plot the location of artifacts in unit B2.

SPECIAL SAMPLES FOR ANALYSIS

Flotation is a recovery method widely used in archaeology that involves dumping samples of soil into water and skimming any floating material off the surface. The material that floats (the "light fraction") is mostly organic and may include charred plant remains as well as tiny bone fragments, fish scales, and so forth. The sediment that settles to the bottom of the flotation unit (the "heavy fraction") is also saved for inspection, as it may contain very tiny fragments of artifacts. Flotation may be done using chemical solutions that help separate the organic material from the sediments or that make the seeds more buoyant.

Following the field season at Nambillo, 83 soil samples of 3 liters each (not the same as the ones used for phosphate analysis) were transported to the Central Bank Museum in Quito, and my same student crew "floated" each sample one by one in water. As we had anticipated, there was no obvious ancient organic material recovered in any of the samples. Some samples, especially those near the modern ground surface, did contain organic matter, but we were able to recognize it as recent, since it was not charred. Only carbonized (charred) organic matter will survive for a long time under good conditions, so that was what we looked for. This apparent absence of old organic material was not surprising for a humid tropical site where even charring is no guarantee that material will be preserved for centuries. It would have been preferable to hire a paleoethnobotanist (an archaeologist or botanist who specializes in the identification of ancient botanical remains) to do a microscopic study of several of the samples, but we were unable to obtain funding for such a study and were certain that very little identifiable material would turn up, anyway.

A few other soil samples were saved for pollen analysis. Each species of plant produces pollen grains of a distinctive shape, so that palynologists can identify the plants that were formerly prevalent in the area. In turn, this information helps them to reconstruct the climate at the time of occupation. Conditions at the site such as wet-dry soil cycles and high soil microbial activity conspire against pollen preservation. When we sent a few samples to a palynologist in Ecuador for inspection, he found them not to contain enough pollen to be useful, so we did not request funding for a full-scale study.

From one of the finished test pits, I collected a series of tephra samples from different strata and depths and sent these volcanic sediments off to an archaeologist in Illinois, John Isaacson, who has done mineralogical work correlating different kinds of tephra with various volcanic eruptions in northern Ecuador. He made provisional identifications, but once again no funding was available to pay for a detailed, definitive analysis.[3] The fact that he did a small amount of free work for us is not at all unusual. Archaeologists and other scientists frequently provide limited services at no charge because we all understand the difficulties of obtaining adequate funding. Besides, even a cursory analysis is usually useful to the specialist who is compiling samples of data from various sites. One of the great challenges of nearly all archaeological projects is optimizing recovery and analysis given drastic budget limitations.

FEATURES DISCOVERED

Archaeologists use the word *feature* to refer to any construction or disturbance at the site that was made by the ancient inhabitants or by anyone else before the archaeologists began their work. Despite the fact that vertical excavations are not ideal for uncovering habitation features, we did in fact come across a few features during the excavation of the six test pits. One of these features looked like a large hearth that was partially within excavation unit B2. The distinctive light gray ashy area was partly demarcated by a small rock and two large sherds (Figure 6.3). The nearly spherical rock and one of the two sherds seemed to have been placed purposely at the perimeter of the hearth to help contain the ash. The fire pit was fairly large for a household cooking fire, but that seems to have been the most likely function.

We could not excavate the rest of the hearth to get more information about it because it would have taken too long and would have diverted us from our primary objective of doing test pits for chronological information. To excavate the entire feature properly and to maximize information, we would have had to excavate an entirely new test pit adjacent to the one on which we were working in order to come down on the hearth from above. A shortcut consisting of burrowing into the adjacent square sideways at the level of the hearth would have been highly destructive; such a procedure is never allowed in archaeological method except under extreme salvage

---

[3]The results of the provisional analysis will be discussed in Chapter 9.

Figure 6.3 Feature 3 showing large area of ashy sediment in eastern part of unit B2 and small round rock at edge of ash (at upper right corner of sign). A large sherd also at the edge of the ash was removed prior to this photograph (from just above the "18" on the sign) and a second sherd was later found within the ashy sediment.

conditions. Future excavations should reveal more about the feature and place it in context within a habitation site.

Another feature was half in unit B1 and half in B2. Feature 1 was a shallow circular pit that has been interpreted as a small garbage pit. Refuse found concentrated in the small hole includes several large and small sherds, flecks of charcoal, a small fired ball of clay, a basalt flake, and other lithic debris of obsidian and chert (a rock similar to flint). It is very commonplace at village sites to find that refuse was often disposed of by placing it in holes and then covering it over with dirt. As we carefully excavated the contents of the pit, a very small whitish object was found that we at first believed was an animal molar. However, at first touch with a dental pick, the tooth—if that is what it really was—practically disintegrated before our eyes. Given how fragile it was, it seems unlikely it was actually a tooth. What very little of it we were able to put in a vial could not be subsequently identified by a specialist. This sort of occurrence demonstrates yet another kind of frustration involved in tropical forest archaeology!

A third and final feature worth commenting on here contained the only definite bone found at the site (Figure 6.4). This was a well-preserved femur (lower leg bone) of an equine—either a horse or donkey. The bone was discovered within the fifth excavated level of Paleosol 1 in excavation unit B2. It was found in association with a few sherds but was not part of an occupation floor. On one of our weekend trips back to Quito, we took the bone to a university and had it identified by a zoologist. The pronouncement that it belonged to a horse or donkey was significant and surprising because such animals did not exist in recent millennia in the Americas but were brought over the Atlantic by the Spanish. This was the only indication during

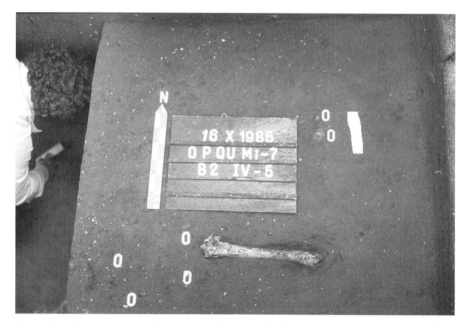

Figure 6.4 Horse or donkey femur in situ *(in its original discard location) in Stratum IV, level 5, of excavation unit B2. Each plastic "O" denotes location of a potsherd. The light specks in the soil are pumice stone.*

our work at Nambillo that there had been some occupation at the site after the Spanish Conquest, which occurred in 1532.

The presence of this lone piece of evidence of Spanish contact created quite a dilemma in our interpretation of the stratigraphy and dating within Paleosol 1. The reason is that radiocarbon dates from higher up in Paleosol 1 were earlier than 1532, and the pottery and other tools appeared to be of indigenous origin with no other evidence of a Spanish presence. One possibility was that the radiocarbon dates were, for some reason, inaccurate and should have been around or after 1532. However, since the dates, when taken together, provided a coherent series from the bottom to the top of Paleosol 1 (see the next section) and since the samples had been large enough and apparently uncontaminated, we had little reason to suspect they were erroneous by several centuries. We also knew the bone was not deposited after 1660, since the site was covered in that year by the yellow sandy tephra of Stratum II. Any hole cut through that sediment would have been very conspicuous.

One might also suggest there is the possibility either that not all equines had become extinct in the Americas at the end of the Ice Age thousands of years earlier or that the bone was evidence of transoceanic contact prior to the Spanish voyages of the early 1500s. Both of these seem extremely unlikely given the absence of corroborating evidence from elsewhere in the Americas.[4] Much more likely, it seems to us, is the possibility that there had been some disturbance within Paleosol 1 that we had not been able to observe. The paleosol was a very homogeneous black clayey-silty stratum. If some Yumbo, say in the 1540s, had obtained a horse bone from the

[4]Except for a 1,000-year-old Viking site (without horses) in Newfoundland, Canada.

Spanish and decided to bury it in the ground in a hole he dug within the same thick soil horizon, it is unlikely we would be able to detect the disturbance—a hole dug in black silt and filled in with black silt would have been virtually invisible. That explanation seems the most reasonable and has the added advantage that it implies we really made no mistake. As much as we would like to believe it, there remains a touch of uncertainty—a nagging feeling that we may have messed up. Such problems are not at all unusual during the course of fieldwork and subsequent interpretation. What is important is that we acknowledge the possibility we may have missed something rather than gloss over it.

FINISHING THE DIG

Our excavations confirmed that the tephravolcanic sediments—Strata II, V, and VII—were in fact culturally sterile (devoid of artifacts) as we had expected. Only near the boundaries of those layers did we find a very low density of artifacts that could be attributed to the mechanical mixing that almost always occurs within soils due to a variety of causes. In excavating the three paleosols by carefully scraping each stratum away a few millimeters at a time, we were able to isolate a number of the so-called occupation floors previously described. Figure 6.5 illustrates one example of such a concentration of potsherds and lithics (flaked stone artifacts and flaking debris).

Once we were down to the subsoil in the test pit, we performed small probes into that very hard substrate to confirm that it was, almost literally, rock bottom. The excavation was then complete, and considerable time was spent diagramming in detail the stratigraphy that was visible in each of the four walls of the pit. Figure 6.6 shows one of the Ecuadorian students mapping the strata, and Figure 6.7 is an example of two completed wall profile diagrams. During the subsequent analysis of materials, the excavation level forms were constantly checked against the wall profile diagrams to make certain that the stratum association of each artifact was clear and that no recording errors had been made. When an error was found, which happened infrequently, the artifacts in question were put into a pile of artifacts of uncertain provenience, so as not to put them into the wrong stratum. It is always important to be conservative rather than risk an error of association.

The final task was to backfill each excavation unit. The primary purpose of filling in the pits at Nambillo was to protect the undisturbed surrounding areas of the site from collapse and erosion. At sites that are not so isolated from daily human activity, backfilling has the added advantages of discouraging looting and preventing dangerous falls by curious visitors. At this remote jungle location, the only visitor to fall in one of our holes was an armadillo.[5]

Initial fieldwork, including mapping, clearing of vegetation, and soil coring, had begun in late August, and the excavation season came to an end by late January due to increased rainfall. Not only was fieldwork getting more unpleasant and complicated due to the rain, but a couple of landslides along the dirt road leading from Mindo to Nambillo made access to the site too difficult and dangerous. The day I decided to end the field season was the day our vehicle got stuck in mud on the way

---

[5]Since they are burrowing animals, it was able to tunnel its way back to the surface and escape before we returned to work the next day.

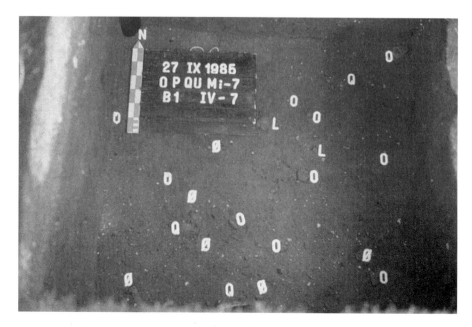

Figure 6.5 This is an example (Stratum IV, level 7, unit B1) of a presumed occupation floor denoted by the concentration in a horizontal plane of various sherds and lithic artifacts. Since artifacts are hard to see in the photograph, plastic yellow symbols were used to show their locations. Sherds are denoted by "0," "O," or "Q," and lithics (flaked stone) by "L." The "N" above the arrow denotes north. Immediately to the left of the "N" a soil coring hole is visible at the corner of this 1 m × 1 m excavation unit.

to the site and we slid around quite a bit trying to extricate ourselves. The vehicle finally came to rest at the left edge of the dirt road. When I opened my door to get out and survey the situation, I found that I could not step out of the driver's side without falling several hundred feet almost straight down. That was not the closest call we had with vehicles and muddy roads, but I will not share the other stories, since I do not want to upset my wife and kids when they read this book.

RADIOCARBON DATING OF THE SITE

Charcoal was carefully collected any time it was spotted during the excavations, and we ended up with a total of 42 samples. The Museum of the Central Bank agreed to fund up to 15 samples for radiocarbon dating, which at that time (late 1980s) cost about $200 to $250 per sample. Accordingly, I chose 15 samples and shipped them off to a radiocarbon laboratory in the United States, since Ecuador had not yet established its first ^{14}C lab. After several weeks of waiting, the lab provided us with the results, which are tabulated in Table 6.1. The table first lists the laboratory's identification numbers. The provenience is listed by excavation unit, followed by the stratum number (Roman numerals) and the excavation level within the stratum. For example, sample GX-12474 is from the second level of the fourth stratum (Paleosol 1) of excavation unit number 2 on Hill A. The exact (piece-plotted) provenience of that sample is not given here, but could be looked up in the field notes.

Figure 6.6 Oswel Bahamonde carefully draws the wall profile of excavation unit B1 using the mapping grid and a tape measure. His left foot is perched on a step cut into a balsa log that was used as a ladder.

The next column gives the estimated age in radiocarbon years along with the standard deviation. Rather than launching into a lengthy explanation of the significance of these numbers, suffice it to say that a "radiocarbon year" is not precisely the same length as a solar year. Radiocarbon years differ from solar years due to variations over time in the ratio of $^{14}C/^{12}C$, which in turn is due to such phenomena as fluctuations in the earth's magnetic field, increases in the use of fossil fuels, and the testing of nuclear weapons in the atmosphere. Radiocarbon specialists have found a way of using tree rings of known age to correct ("calibrate") the radiocarbon years so that they are virtually the same as actual solar years. The calibrated date is shown in the following two columns.

The standard deviation reflects the fact that radiocarbon labs cannot measure the exact value of the ratio, but can measure only within a certain range. The standard deviation is calculated by a normal distribution method frequently used by statisticians such that there is, in the next to last column, a 68.2% probability that the actual date of the charcoal falls within the range of one standard deviation. The final column shows an even greater range obtained by doubling the standard deviation to raise the confidence level to 95.4%. A basic archaeology text will explain this statistical process as well as the theoretical underpinnings more fully. What is important

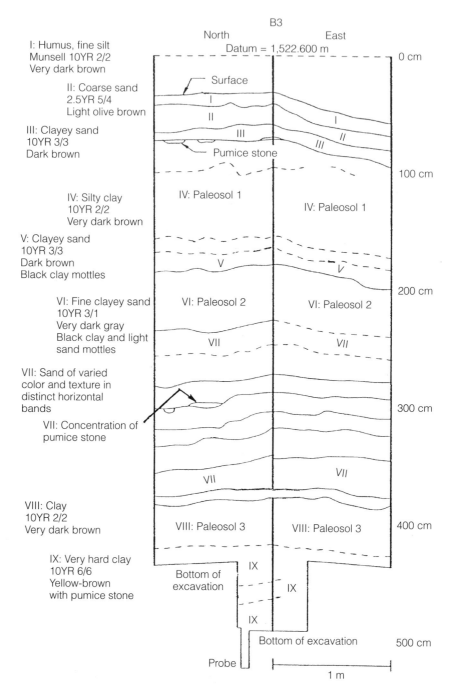

I: Humus, fine silt
Munsell 10YR 2/2
Very dark brown

II: Coarse sand
2.5YR 5/4
Light olive brown

III: Clayey sand
10YR 3/3
Dark brown

IV: Silty clay
10YR 2/2
Very dark brown

V: Clayey sand
10YR 3/3
Dark brown
Black clay mottles

VI: Fine clayey sand
10YR 3/1
Very dark gray
Black clay and light
sand mottles

VII: Sand of varied
color and texture in
distinct horizontal
bands

VII: Concentration of
pumice stone

VIII: Clay
10YR 2/2
Very dark brown

IX: Very hard clay
10YR 6/6
Yellow-brown
with pumice stone

B3
North   East
Datum = 1,522.600 m   0 cm

Surface

I

II

III

I

II

III

Pumice stone

100 cm

IV: Paleosol 1   IV: Paleosol 1

V   V

200 cm

VI: Paleosol 2   VI: Paleosol 2

VII   VII

300 cm

VII   VII

VIII: Paleosol 3   VIII: Paleosol 3   400 cm

IX

Bottom of
excavation   IX

IX

Bottom of excavation   500 cm

Probe

1 m

Figure 6.7 Diagram of the north and east wall profiles of excavation unit B3. Solid lines indicate well-defined boundaries, whereas broken lines show more tenuous boundaries.

TABLE 6.1   RADIOCARBON DATA FOR 15 CHARCOAL SAMPLES FROM NAMBILLO

Lab. No.	Provenience	C-14 Age Rcybp*	Calibration** 1 St. Dev. (68.2%)	Calibration** 2 St. Dev. (95.4%)
Paleosol 1				
GX-12474	A2 IV-2	1015 +/- 130	A.D. 890–1170	A.D. 700–1300
GX-12475	B2 IV-3	820 +/- 75	8%: A.D. 1050–1080 / 92%: A.D. 1120–1280	A.D. 1030–1280
GX-12476	B2 IV-4	895 +/- 75	A.D. 1040–1200	A.D. 1010–1270
GX-12477	D1 IV-6	995 +/- 70	A.D. 970–1160	A.D. 890–1200
GX-12478	B1 IV-7 & B2 IV-7	905 +/- 130	A.D. 1010–1240	A.D. 850–1400
GX-12479	A2 IV-7	1665 +/- 75	A.D. 250–450	A.D. 200–560
Paleosol 2				
GX-12466	A2 VI-1	1775 +/- 75	A.D. 140–340	A.D. 80–420
GX-12467	D1 VI-2	1665 +/- 200	A.D. 140–590	150 B.C.–A.D. 800
GX-12465	B3 VI-2	2095 +/- 80	9%: 350–320 B.C. / 91%: 210–1 B.C.	370 B.C.–A.D. 60
GX-12468	D1 VI-3 (Feature 8)	2515 +/- 85	20%: 800–750 B.C. / 80%: 730–520 B.C.	810–400 B.C.
Paleosol 3				
GX-12469	A2 VIII-2 & B3 VIII-2	3225 +/- 260	1900–1150 B.C.	2200–800 B.C.
GX-12470	B3 VIII-3	4540 +/- 80	3370–3100 B.C.	3550–2900 B.C.
GX-12471	A2 VIII-3	5325 +/- 110	15%: 4330–4280 B.C. / 85%: 4250–4040 B.C.	4450–3950 B.C.
GX-12472	B1 VIII-5	2315 +/- 260	800–100 B.C.	1100 B.C.–A.D. 300
GX-12473	B2 VIII-5	3330 +/- 80	6%: 1740–1720 B.C. / 94%: 1700–1520 B.C.	4%: 1880–1840 B.C. / 1%: 1820–1800 B.C. / 95%: 1780–1440 B.C.

*"rcybp" (radiocarbon years before present) dates are based on the Libby half-life of 5,570 years. These dates have been corrected, when necessary, for high C-13 values.
**Calibrations were done using the OxCal software (Ramsey 1995), which is based on tables created by M. Stuiver and R. S. Kra (1986).

to keep in mind is that radiocarbon dates are, even when calibrated using the tree ring data, estimates within a specified range; they are never exact dates.

"One radiocarbon date is no radiocarbon dates" is an axiom of archaeology. The purpose of this seemingly nonsensical expression is to emphasize that there are a number of kinds of errors that can creep into radiocarbon analysis. One way to minimize the probability of certain errors is never to rely upon a single date or a very few dates but to have a whole series of dates that show stratigraphic coherency. That explains why we were willing to spend quite a bit of money for 15 dates, even though we had other kinds of analyses we wanted done but could not afford.

To illustrate more clearly that the radiocarbon dates, which represented various levels in all three paleosols, are approximately in the order one would expect (youngest at the top and oldest at the bottom), the dates have been graphed in stratigraphic order in Figure 6.8. The tiny curvilinear figures accompanying each date represent the actual probability distributions for each calibration; for our purposes, we can ignore the details of those distributions and focus on the left and right extreme of the curve for each date. It is clear that the dates for Paleosol 1 are all roughly contemporary except for the date from the lowest level, which is slightly older, as we would expect. This suggests that the various occupations associated with Paleosol 1 occurred in fairly quick succession, or perhaps even continuously. For Paleosol 2, the four dates get older from top to bottom, as is usually the case.

Paleosol 3 is a little more problematic, since the five dates within that stratum are not in the expected sequence. This is fairly strong evidence that there were disturbances within Paleosol 3 that we did not observe during the excavations. Moreover, two of the dates from Paleosol 3 (GX-12469 and GX-12472) have very large standard deviations, indicating that they are very imprecise dates. Overall, it is reassuring that the dates from one paleosol to the next are in stratigraphic sequence. Given the thick, sterile volcanic sediments separating them, it would have been quite surprising were this not the case. A more detailed analysis of these dates will be done in Chapter 9 to compare them with radiocarbon dates from other archaeological complexes in surrounding regions of Ecuador.

CONCLUSIONS REGARDING THE RESEARCH AT NAMBILLO

The studies of the stratigraphy at Nambillo, both from the soil coring and the test excavations (Figure 6.9), provide a very good chronological sequence for the site and a tentative "master sequence" for the entire region. Not only do we now have clear evidence of three separate episodes of prehistoric occupations, but we also have samples of pottery and stone tools from each episode and are able to date those three periods, thanks to the radiocarbon assays. While there undoubtedly is some variability in local chronologies throughout Western Pichincha, we can compare the pottery found in other localities of the region or beyond to pieces excavated at Nambillo and perform cross-dating. That is, we can determine the contemporaneity of sites by the presence of the same kinds of pottery. Because virtually all of Western Pichincha was affected, to one degree or another, by the same major volcanic eruptions, it is likely that the overall division of regional prehistory into these three principal periods is fairly uniform. We are fortunate that natural disasters provide us with convenient timelines for studying the regional chronology (more fortunate than the Yumbos,

Nambillo C14

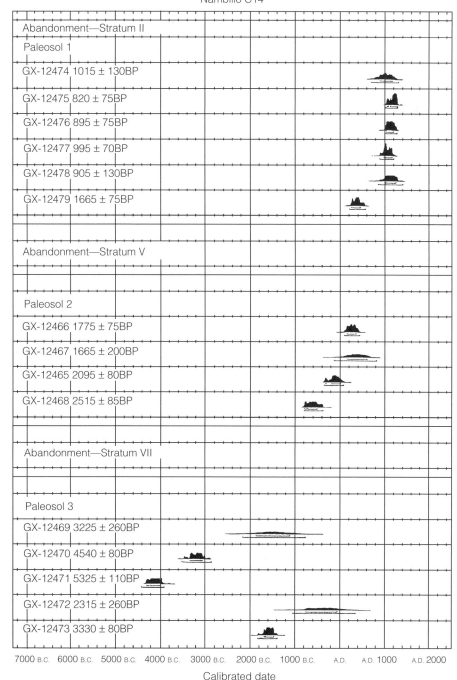

Figure 6.8 Graph of radiocarbon calibrations presented in stratigraphic order. The wider the calibration curve, the more imprecise the date. The uncalibrated laboratory dates are given to the left.

I: Humus

II: A.D. 1660 tephra deposit

III: Transition

IV: Paleosol 1

V: Tephra deposits

VI: Paleosol 2

VII: Deep tephra deposits

VIII: Paleosol 3

IX: Subsoil base

Figure 6.9 The wall profile of excavation unit B3. Since the unit was only 1 m wide and over 4 m deep, the picture had to be taken from above looking downward. This causes a foreshortening of the various strata, especially the lower ones. The three paleosols are labeled as well as the other strata. The two apparent light bands within Paleosol 1 are not lighter soil but rather are bands where the vertical wall protruded a little and reflected the camera flash. A bamboo ladder appears at the extreme lower part of the photograph.

Niguas, and their predecessors, who had to live through these catastrophes). This matter of chronology will be presented in more detail in Chapter 9.

Because we did not perform more extensive excavations, especially horizontal excavations of living floors, we can do little more than speculate about the climate of each period, the diet of the inhabitants, the population of the settlements, the nature of their exchange system, and so many other aspects of their cultures. Nonetheless, the chronological evidence is what we were after for that all-too-brief field season, and we were quite successful in meeting our goal. These other matters will need to be addressed in future work.

The following two chapters return to the survey data, now placed within this chronological context, and show how interpretations proceeded from the data accumulated. By Chapter 9 we will work toward a tentative reconstruction, based partly on inference from evidence and partly on educated guesses, of the lives and times of these long-vanished peoples.

7/Lost and Found— Special Interest Sites

CATALOGED ARCHAEOLOGICAL SITES

In Chapter 4 a map was presented (Figure 4.3) showing the actual survey transects within Western Pichincha. Two hundred ninety-three archaeological sites have been discovered and catalogued so far along those transects since the beginning of the Western Pichincha Project. However, there is relatively little that can be said of most of those sites. A modest amount of sherds (pottery fragments) and/or lithics (stone tools and associated debris) was collected from most of them and the actual size and nature of the sites is generally undetermined. At best for many of those sites we can estimate their approximate age by cross-dating with Nambillo pottery or pottery known from other parts of Ecuador. This may help us relate sites to one or another culture area. That is, it may be possible to define the spatial and temporal limits of certain nations or ethnic groups based on the distribution of pottery types. We will return to this sort of reconstruction in chapters 8–9. In the present chapter, I discuss briefly those sites where particular kinds of structures or other features were found so that some general statements about special kinds of sites can help us in understanding the ancient inhabitants.

TOLAS—ARTIFICIAL EARTHEN MOUNDS

In many parts of Ecuador there is a variety of tola complexes consisting of earthen structures of different forms, sizes, ages and—presumably—functions. These features almost certainly represent specific ideologies, perhaps religious and/or political. By their very size, the larger mounds imply the mobilization of a large and well-organized labor force as well as planning and design by knowledgeable specialists. Consequently, the presence of large earthen mounds has traditionally suggested to archaeologists the existence of at least a moderately complex sociocultural system, possibly at the level that anthropologists usually identify as a tribe or, more likely, a chiefdom.

The existence of very abundant and impressive tolas in the northern highlands of Ecuador was already mentioned in Chapter 3. There are also mound complexes of a different sort in the northern coastal province of Esmeraldas. Farther south along the coast toward the Gulf of Guayaquil, there are more mound complexes that seem still different from the others. Finally, in the eastern lowlands of Ecuador (the "Orient" or Upper Amazon), mound complexes have also come to light in the last few decades. Since the pioneering study of Tulipe by Salomon and Erickson (1984), mentioned in Chapter 2, revealed the existence of mounds in Western Pichincha, we were not particularly surprised to come across some. When Isaacson (1982) followed up on their brief work with a more systematic survey of mounds in the Tulipe zone, he counted an impressive total of eighty-six mounds within an area of only 50 km^2.

As our survey moved forward, we found a variety of earthen mounds in Western Pichincha outside the Tulipe zone, but the density of mounds was never close to what Isaacson had found. This was probably in part because the Tulipe zone had been mostly deforested in previous decades by ranchers whereas we worked more in areas where mounds would still be hidden in the rainforest and difficult to discover. Despite this difference in visibility, I have gravitated toward the tentative conclusion that the Tulipe zone probably really does have a higher density of mounds than is found elsewhere in the region; all of our surveying elsewhere simply did not turn up as many mounds.

Once we started observing tolas, we made concerted efforts to find more. This involved careful observation of the landscape and some help from local residents. Much more often than not, the willingness of the local people to help us turned out not to be so valuable. Despite our efforts to explain carefully what we meant by tolas, we were usually taken to "tolas" that contained nothing even remotely similar to artificial earthen mounds. It turned out that the local dialect used *"tola"* to refer to any presumed ancient burial grounds or to certain places where something "weird" had once been observed, and most people who do not study the landscape for a living have great difficulty distinguishing between natural and artificial mounds.

In one instance we did not discover a very large rectangular platform mound near Mindo until after a few months of passing it each day on foot or in a vehicle. This impressive structure (at Mi-9) was situated just alongside the dirt road that led from Mindo to the Nambillo site. During our first trips to Mindo and the early stages of fieldwork at Nambillo, the tola was completely hidden in dense vegetation. Some time later, the local landowner began turning the site into pasture and the mound stood out as plain as day. A few years later, we discovered another complex of at least four platform mounds (Mi-19) on a hill just a kilometer or so past this mound; those newly discovered tolas had remained invisible until more land was cleared. How many other mounds were missed by us because of the forest cover and our necessarily spotty surveying methods cannot be estimated, though I still am inclined to believe that the density of mounds is nowhere as great as around Tulipe.

Since archaeological work often results in lots of mysterious finds, let me digress for a moment to tell of an interesting reported phenomenon in the region. In many localities throughout Western Pichincha we were informed over and over again by local residents that at night they sometimes observe blue flames emanating from the ground where there are mounds. The explanation in the local folklore is that precious metals—silver is usually stipulated—are buried in the mounds and their decomposition causes these flames to appear. Neither my crewmembers nor I ever observed this phenomenon firsthand, but the repeated reports of it intrigued us even if the folk explanation seemed very unlikely.

If one looks for a scientific explanation, a possibility is that the flames are the combustion of methane gas produced by the decomposition of cadavers in the mounds. However, cadavers that are centuries old are already reduced to nothing but bone, so it seems there should not be much residual methane. And then one could ask what causes the gas to ignite. Given the slightly different local usage of "*tola*" than we were used to in archaeology, we were not able to ascertain whether these purported flames were really associated with mounds or whether people just assumed that there were mounds or burials wherever they saw such flames; I think the latter explanation is more likely. It is well known that flickering luminescence can often be seen over marshes at night and this is attributed to the spontaneous combustion of the methane ("marsh gas") produced through vegetal decomposition. In English such a phenomenon is known as will-o'-the-wisp. I suppose there is also the possibility of some sort of static electricity "glow discharge"; this is a well-known phenomenon usually referred to as St. Elmo's fire. The electrical discharge during stormy weather runs to a high point, such as a church steeple or ship's mast. Neither the will-o'-the-wisp nor St. Elmo's fire seems similar to what so many people reported to us. While we have neither direct evidence of such a phenomenon nor a compelling explanation of it, I enjoy a good mystery and consider such enigma to be a bonus when doing archaeological fieldwork.

Platform Mounds

The mounds that were discovered were classified, as others have done in the past, on the basis of their form and size. The largest mounds generally were the rectangular flat-topped mounds with straight, steeply sloped sides and often having one or two ramps of access to the top platform (Figure 7.1). These are variously called platform mounds, temple mounds, pyramidal mounds or, simply, pyramids, though they are really only truncated pyramids.

Pyramidal mounds are well known and abundant in the northern highlands of Ecuador in association with the Caranqui culture area, as discussed in Chapter 3. The pyramids of Western Pichincha are similar but not identical in form to those of Caranqui, as can be seen in Figure 7.2, which shows the Caranqui pyramids often having very long, tapering ramps. Although I am certain that there are many more such mounds yet to be discovered in Western Pichincha, a distribution map of those already catalogued (Figure 7.3) proved quite interesting. This map shows a zone of platform mounds running southwest across the region from the Guayllabamba River at the northern boundary nearly to the Toachi River at the southern extreme. Following these mounds northeastward across the Guayllabamba, there is a more or less continuous distribution of them to the highland Caranqui country (see Figure 3.1). Where such mounds have been excavated in the Caranqui sierra north of Quito, they have been found to contain only an occasional incidental burial but to have served primarily as earthen platforms upon which temples or large houses were built.

I was also interested in analyzing the size and orientation of these mounds trying to find some pattern. Scientists search for patterns in their data and statistics provides a number of techniques for recognizing such patterns. Without statistical techniques, one is reduced to making simple observations that may or may not be real or typical. All people commonly make such observations, but unless the observations are rigorous and the analysis statistical in nature, the patterns may be illusions or merely

Figure 7.1 Platform mound of Ilambo (Nt-7) clearly visible following deforestation

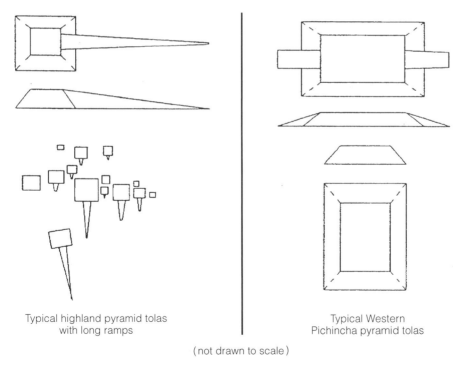

Typical highland pyramid tolas
with long ramps

Typical Western
Pichincha pyramid tolas

(not drawn to scale)

*Figure 7.2 Comparison of Yumbo (Western Pichincha) and Caranqui (north highland)
platform or pyramidal mounds*

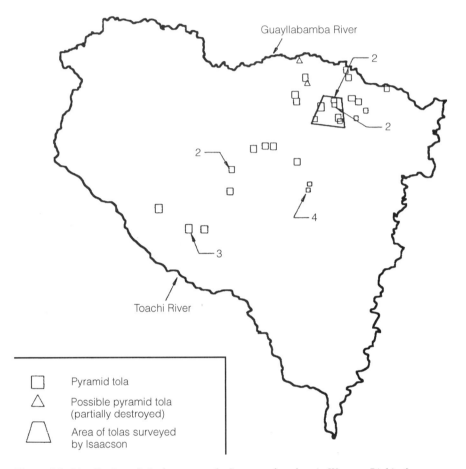

Figure 7.3 Distribution of platform mounds discovered to date in Western Pichincha

coincidental. Accordingly, I employed some very basic statistical procedures to find any sort of "rules" that seemed to have been shared by the mound builders through-out the region. A few of those simple procedures are briefly described below.

Thirty-five platform mounds were catalogued during our surveys that were in a good enough state of preservation to allow fairly accurate measurements to be taken. The basic measurements were made of the upper surface (platform) since this was usually well defined, whereas the base of the mound often blended somewhat smoothly into the undulating landscape or may have been eroded. The measurements of the platform included length, width and average height above the surrounding ter-rain. The smallest of the truncated pyramids was a mere 8.5 m × 5 m and stood about 1 m high. The largest was 62 m × 20 m (more than half the size of a football or soc-cer field) and rose approximately 7 m above the surrounding plain. I tried graphing the dimensions to determine whether there were certain sizes that appeared to be favored, but the graphs failed to show any obvious size patterns (see Figure 7.4, for example). If one looks at these graphs (of length, width and length/width), the bars do not show any clear tendencies in size but rather a seemingly random assortment of sizes. The only pattern that was forthcoming at all was with respect to the ratio of

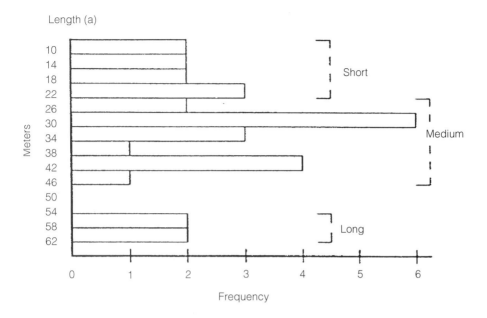

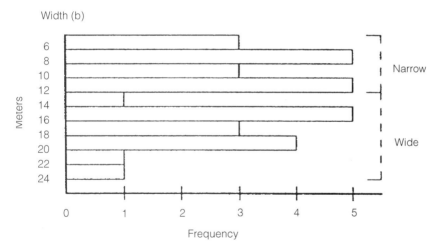

Figure 7.4 Histograms of length and width of platform mounds showing no definite size preference

the length and width. It was found that there was a tendency for the length to be approximately two and one half times the width. These measurements are graphed in Figure 7.5, in which the broken line represents a statistical estimate of the average ratio (known to statisticians as a linear regression). The scattered plots on the graph show that the ratio was not perfectly adhered to (or they would all fall along the broken line) but that it seems to be close to the ideal for such structures. It is one thing to find such a consistent ratio but quite another to determine the reason for it.

It was also noted whether or not the platform mound had an access ramp or two by graphing the height of the mound against the presence or absence of ramps. Here

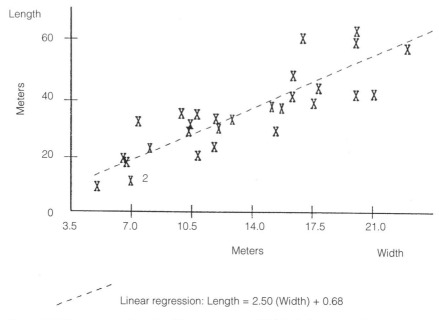

Figure 7.5 *Linear regression plot of length versus width of platform mounds*

the result was not surprising: the taller mounds usually had one or two ramps whereas the lower mounds usually lacked them. This makes sense in that the lower mounds were easy to ascend without a special ramp while the taller ones were too steep. It is possible that the ramps were enhanced by the addition of log steps, though that is speculative since any wood used long ago would not survive to modern times.

Another analysis involved graphing the orientation of each ramp with regard to the cardinal directions. We recorded with a compass the bearing of the long axis of each mound and then plotted these readings in what is known as a "rosette diagram." It can be seen from this illustration (Figure 7.6) that there appears to have been no attempt to orient the mound in any particular direction, for example, in the direction of the rising sun. I suspect the orientation was more a matter of the local terrain than any widely shared ideology about the proper way to align the mound.

Various other statistical analyses were done using computer software to find other patterns in the mounds. Another variable considered besides those already mentioned was elevation above sea level. Again, there were no additional significant patterns discovered, suggesting that even though the practice of building pyramidal mounds was widespread, the actual "rules" for its construction were highly variable.

Round Mounds

The other major group of tolas varied from nearly hemispherical to subconical (Figure 7.7), though sometimes the ground plan was oblong rather than round. This type of mound is found in various parts of Ecuador and is usually considered a burial mound. These are often tricky to identify positively in the field since they can sometimes be confused with natural hillocks. We learned to be fairly conservative in cataloguing these mounds after more careful observation or coring showed some of

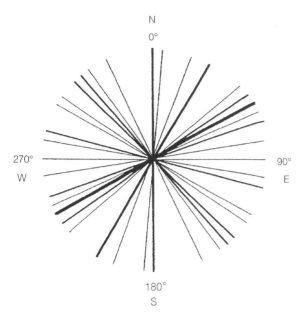

N
0°

270°
W

90°
E

180°
S

Figure 7.6 Rosette diagram of orientation of long axis of platform mounds showing no preferred alignment. The thicker radial lines indicate that two or three mounds had the same orientation.

Figure 7.7 Large round mound (SD-14, no.2) easily visible in clearing. Two students can barely be seen climbing the mound toward the right side.

the "round mounds" were actually natural elevations. Coring a mound using a soil probe will show unnatural fill deposits that differ from the natural soil stratigraphy near the mounds; on the other hand, natural hillocks will usually contain the natural layering of soil horizons and sediments for that locality. The mounds described in this section are quite definitely artificial mounds.

The first analytical step was to graph the mounds by size, in this case using the diameter and the approximate height. Again, the measurements were not always exact due to erosion, partial destruction, or the gradual blending of the base of the mound into the natural landscape. Despite these measurement problems, the graph showed a definite bimodal ("two-humped") pattern (Figure 7.8). A large number of mounds measured from 2 m to 8 m in diameter and another cluster of mounds measured approximately 20 m in diameter. There were no mounds that fell in between those two modes. This allowed us to subdivide the round mounds into small and large ones in a completely non-arbitrary way since it appeared that the mound-builders had intended to create mounds in two distinct sizes (leaving open the possibility that the two sizes were built at different times or by different peoples).

The small ones we chose to refer to as *tumuli* (singular is *tumulus*), which is a Latin term commonly used in European archaeology for small burial mounds. Tumuli were discovered in three different situations: a few near a pyramidal mound, one or two in apparent isolation, and many in large cemetery complexes. The cemetery complexes consisted of a dozen or more small mounds tightly clustered together on a mountaintop. It is quite certain that these small mounds generally, if not always, are burial mounds since a few of them had been previously looted by treasure hunters. There apparently were no treasures to be found; otherwise, the entire complex of mounds would have been dug up. However, there were human bone fragments in poor condition as well as large potsherds of red-painted jugs. These jugs are believed to have contained *chicha,* a native beer made of fermented corn mash, since that was a widespread Andean tradition, and in fact, some inhabitants declared that they had actually excavated whole sealed jugs that still contained *chicha.* We found two examples of such mountaintop cemeteries, and we had reliable reports from trusted informants of three other sites, though we were not able to reach those sites on our own. The tumuli were typically about 3–4 m in diameter and roughly 1 m high. One of the two cemeteries that we visited was quite remote and had, therefore, been subjected to very little looting. We counted fifty-seven well-preserved round mounds on the summit of the mountain and believe there were more that were not easily found in the forest vegetation.

FORTS

Up and down the Andes, military sites of Inca origin are known by their Quichua name *pucará*. It is possible that some of these sites may have been locally built to defend against the Inca advance. Still others might have been pre-Inca sites but were taken over by the Inca army as it expanded its empire northward. Previous research in the highlands has not resolved this issue to our satisfaction regarding the identity of the original builders. All that can be said is that if a fair amount of Inca pottery is found at these forts, then they are presumed to have been Inca forts at least during their final occupation. These are hilltop sites often having two or more concentric stone walls that conform to the natural relief and may contain evidence of small stone masonry structures at the summit. The hillsides are often modified into large step-like terraces with stone-faced retaining walls. These defensive terraces are common in the northern Ecuadorian highlands unlike agricultural terraces, which are almost unknown there. Pottery is usually a mixture of local styles and Inca wares. As discussed in Chapter 3, the Inca expansion in Ecuador was primarily through the

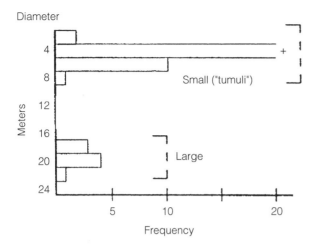

Figure 7.8 Histogram of diameters of round mounds showing clear bimodal size distribution

Andean highlands and not, so far as was thought, with much success in either the eastern or western lowlands. Since early Spanish documents made vague references to Inca roads through Western Pichincha and since maps contain a few place names that refer specifically to the Inca (*"Inga"* in 16th century Spanish), we suspected there might be archaeological evidence of Inca intrusion into the montaña of Western Pichincha.

Early on we were successful at finding two previously unknown forts, probably Inca, at two of the mountain passes where one begins the descent into Western Pichincha. These discoveries were not surprising since the Incas made a lot of effort to control the movement of peoples and goods into their domain. Figure 7.9 shows the grass-covered hill of Portalanza, where we discovered terraces and masonry retaining walls of a fort most likely of Inca origin. The Portalanza fort guards the deep Guayllabamba River canyon and is located in a strategic position to control traders and potential raiders.

It was quite a bit more surprising to find two probable Inca forts in the rainforest habitat well within Western Pichincha. The fort at Palmitopamba[1] occupies a high hill overlooking a vast plateau just south of the Guayllabamba River; it is visible as a series of terraces, but more careful inspection revealed stone-faced retaining walls and a smattering of Inca pottery. Just a few kilometers away is another fort inside the Guayllabamba River canyon. This second fort at a village called Chacapata (meaning "bridge abutments" in Quichua) is located on a knoll immediately next to the river at a point where rock outcrops narrow the river width to just a few meters, making it an ideal place to build a bridge. At this rainforest site there was evidence of the concentric walls and of small masonry structures at the center. The site has been a sugarcane plantation in recent years. The first time we visited the ruins was after the harvest when the field had been cleared by burning. It was possible to produce a reasonable sketch map at that time. All subsequent visits to the site occurred when the tall, dense sugarcane made the site nearly impenetrable and it was much more difficult to visualize the fort layout. The sketch map is shown in Figure 7.10 and a view of a stonewall in Figure 7.11. A recent field season was dedicated to precise mapping

---

[1]We began excavations at the Palmitopamba pucará in the summer of 2002 as this book was going to press.

Figure 7.9 Grass-covered fortress of Portalanza (Cc-37) with defensive terraces visible

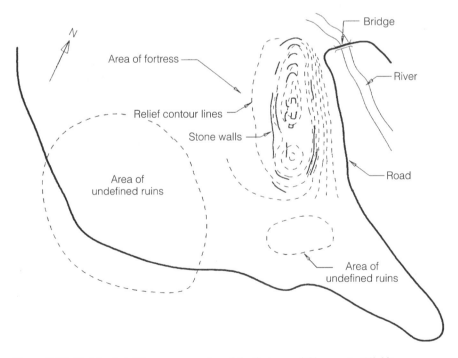

Figure 7.10 Sketch of visible masonry ruins of the fortress of Chacapata (Nl-13)

Figure 7.11 Close-up view of masonry wall at Chacapata (Nl-13). A range pole with 25-cm painted intervals is visible just left of center for scale.

of some of these tola and pucará sites, and that work will continue into the future as a prelude to excavations.

PETROGLYPHS

Petroglyphs are engravings in stone and a few examples of this rock art were found on river boulders in one of the tropical rivers north of Santo Domingo. We found the first set of petroglyphs when they were shown to us by a local inhabitant near his village, and we then spent some time in the region looking for others. Looking for artwork on river boulders was not an easy chore since it involved wading or boulder jumping across and along fast-moving rivers while trying to keep our heads, notebooks, cameras and other equipment dry. On the few boulders that we found with pictures, the designs had been pecked into the rock surface most likely using a stone hammer. The earliest modern inhabitants in the vicinity told us the rock art was there when they first settled a few decades ago, and as far as we know, nobody had lived there in at least the last century. Although we cannot date the engravings, we are very confident they are not modern. We also presume they were not Inca since the images do not fit what is known of Inca iconography. Our best guess is that they were made many centuries ago by the Yumbos or by the Tsáchila prior to the 20th century. Figure 7.12 shows one boulder containing several images.

Early on we were stuck on the interpretations, as so often happens with ancient art, so a few years ago Alfredo Santamaría and I made contact, as discussed at the beginning of this book, with some Tsáchila elders near Santo Domingo in the hope of learning more about the engravings in case they were meaningful symbols for them today. As was discussed in Chapter 3, I believe the Tsáchila formerly lived in the area of these engravings and may have some knowledge of them or at least some understanding of their meaning or function. Even if direct ancestors of the Tsáchila

Figure 7.12 Petroglyphs on a boulder in the Memé River (SD-17). The images have been highlighted with chalk so they are more easily visible in the photograph. There seem to have been additional images that are badly eroded or were never deeply engraved.

did not create the artwork, the Yumbos who formerly lived in the region spoke a language closely related to the language of the Tsáchila (languages of the Barbacoan family) and, therefore, they may share some mythology and iconography in addition to speaking similar languages. As I have been writing this book, I have renewed contact with Santamaría and gotten him to forge ahead once again with interviews of a few Tsáchila elders.

The most frequent symbol on the boulders looks somewhat like a "happy face" figure but in actuality is a circle or rectangle with rounded corners containing three or four smaller circles within it. Given the variation among these simple figures, we don't believe they are always meant to portray faces—happy or otherwise. One contemporary Tsáchila shaman thought two of the face-like images represented a guardian spirit of a shaman and the spirit's face was drawn for protection. He did not speculate on the other face-like images.

All the figures are hard to interpret. By way of example, I call your attention to the image in Figure 7.13 (on a boulder that may have tipped over from its original position). Two shamans interviewed so far by Santamaría suggest that the image is of a fish. It would be stupendous if we could accept that at face value; unfortunately, things are not so simple. For one thing, we cannot be sure that other Tsáchila shaman or elders would interpret the figure the same way—we need independent corroboration. Secondly, it may be that the symbol as originally drawn had a completely different meaning that has been lost over time, perhaps even within the same ethnic group, or that it is unrelated culturally to anything in the Tsáchila cultural tradition. The most we can safely do for now is consider the fish interpretation as a working hypothesis.

Figure 7.13 A petroglyph variously interpreted as a woman, owl, or fish (SD-17)

I first considered the image of Figure 7.13 to be an owl-like woman (tipped over). Prior to the recent interviews, I read up somewhat on Tsáchila mythology looking for legends involving any of these images. Among those stories I came across one about a woman that was turned into an owl by a sorcerer. Could it be that this image represents that mythical figure or is my imagination forcing a correspondence that does not really exist?

While there is no obvious interpretation of these figures, their location in the river may have some importance. I noticed that all of the rock art (we found a total of only six boulders with engravings) occurred in whitewater boulder fields just above deeper portions of the river that were free of above-water boulders. That is, it seems as if the symbols may have been marking calmer pools just downstream. Since these rivers have abundant fish in them, is it possible that the symbols lay claim to rights to fishing pools? That is merely another hypothesis. Perhaps they have some religious or other ideological significance or are merely "art for art's sake." The petroglyphs are very fascinating but seemingly inscrutable.

LOST TOWNS

According to early Spanish documents, there were several Indian settlements in Western Pichincha that continued to be occupied for some time following the Spanish conquest and during the gradual disappearance or assimilation of Yumbos and Niguas. While some prehispanic settlements were abandoned early in the colonial period, others lasted longer and in a couple of cases even grew in size under Spanish domination. One of our original project goals was to combine the Spanish documentary record with archaeological surveying to locate some of these named towns that were eventually abandoned and reclaimed by the forest. To do this we relied on the ethnohistoric work of Salomon (1997), local informants, and both old and recent maps to track down the settlements. Short of the utterly improbable discovery of an archaeological site with a battered welcome sign naming the town, our identifications of these "lost towns" must necessarily be tentative, but here are some that are very likely correct identifications along with a map of their locations (Figure 7.14).

Small but important trading towns were usually located very near the mountain passes that connected the highlands near Quito with the western montaña. Even today these towns still exist, though they are not necessarily in exactly the same location. In the case of Calacalí, the modern town appears to lie directly on top of the remains of a prehispanic and colonial period town that was called by the same name. We were able to discover artifacts from ancient Calacalí simply by surveying the unpaved streets of the little town and by inspecting a number of small ravines, both of which revealed potsherds and flaked stone. Judging by our discoveries, ancient Calacalí was a little larger or at least more spread out than the modern town. We got additional corroborating evidence from local informants who showed us many interesting artifacts they recovered when the government had come in a few years before us and excavated a series of sewer channels under the present-day streets.

Farther south near the Lloa mountain pass, immediately south of Pichincha volcano, sits the modern village of Lloa as well as artifacts signaling an ancient settlement in the same location. Nonetheless, we found evidence of a larger settlement a few kilometers down the Lloa Valley closer to the start of the cloud forest. The fact is that each mountain pass contains a number of ancient habitation sites, some larger than others, and it is not possible to be certain which one is the ancient town named by the Spanish. Perhaps all of them collectively make up the ancient "town." Recall from Chapter 3 that the Yumbos did not really live in nucleated towns (that is, towns that were clearly defined, compact settlements) but rather tended to live in somewhat dispersed communities. Perhaps the town names given by the Spanish did not refer to a particular settlement so much as to a locality that may have contained a number of villages and hamlets of varying size and density.

Just as an example of a cloud forest town, I refer to a settlement that the Spanish called Alanbi. Alambí is the name given to a major river in the region today and we began with the supposition that *Alanbi* and *Alambí* were the same word with slightly changed pronunciation. It is quite common for the "m" and "n" to be interchanged between Spanish and Barbacoan pronunciation and also to change the accented syllable, so this seemed a good supposition. Furthermore, the Spanish document that refers to this town gives us the approximate route through the mountains. By checking both old and recent maps of the area, we identified certain place names referred to along the ancient route. This often works since place names have a tendency to stay in use long after the native language has been replaced with that of the conqueror's. Such is also true in my state of Wisconsin where Indian place names cover modern maps despite the common usage of English for the past 180 years or so.[2] Moreover, we are told by a Spanish writer who traveled in the region that the town of Alanbi was on the east bank of the Alambí River just below a giant bend at a place known to the Spanish as Dos Puentes ("Two Bridges"). The name Dos Puentes can still be found on certain recent maps even though nobody in the area has any mem-

---

[2]My city's name of Wausau means "place far away" in the Anishinaabe (Chippewa) language.

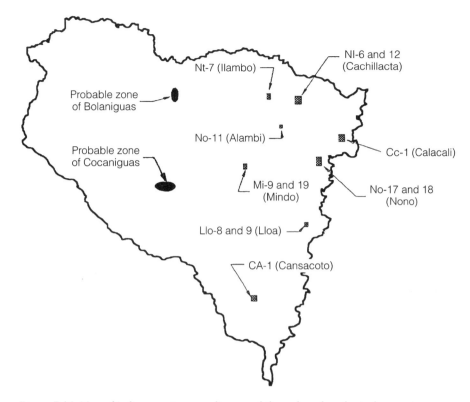

Figure 7.14 Map of indigenous towns rediscovered through archaeological surveying

ory of the old bridges. All of this information suggested where we ought to look for the archaeological remains of Alanbi. Although this locality was very dense cloud forest, a highway was being built there during our survey and we were able to locate in the debris of the highway construction a dense concentration of artifacts from what appeared to have been a fairly sizable village in the same geographic situation described in the text. It is a reasonable conclusion that we found some of the remains of the lost town of Alanbi. We were able to use this same strategy in other parts of Western Pichincha, sometimes with apparent success and other times without.

Perhaps the single most notable accomplishment in this category of discoveries occurred with respect to the ancient town of Cachillacta ("salt town" in Quichua); I briefly mentioned our attention to the word *"cachi"* and our search for a salt mine in Chapter 4. This ancient settlement was particularly important, according to early Spanish records, because Indians exploited salt mines in the vicinity of the town and traded the badly needed mineral to the highlands. Again relying on maps, Spanish documents and local residents, we located briny springs feeding into the Tulambi River next to a mountainside known even today as Cachillacta. On this gently slop-ing mountainside above the salt springs, we were able to locate a sprawling prehis-toric settlement. Finding the settlement was possible because of the recent bulldozer construction of a winding dirt road up the mountainside. In subsequent years, the dirt road was overgrown and it became much more difficult to find artifacts associated with this settlement. The location near salt springs, the size of the habitation site, and the persistence of the name Cachillacta convinced us that this was indeed the ancient salt town. No salt mines have yet been located and, in fact, we suspect that there were no mines, only the salt springs. We intend to collaborate with a geologist in the near future to determine the nature and extent of the salt deposits. The salt could easily be extracted by boiling the salt water in large ceramic bowls. This salt-producing activity apparently continued into fairly recent times, since one older informant told us that his parents had sometimes taken salt from the springs and he even took us to a small rock structure next to one of the springs that had previously been used, judging by the form and heavy soot, as a fireplace for evaporating the salt water. Pottery found higher up in the town of Cachillacta was mostly associated with late prehispanic periods but some of it could be traced all the way back, using the method of cross-dating, to around 1500 B.C., suggesting that the salt trade from Cachillacta had been important for a few millennia.

Two other "lost towns" of special significance were referred to as Bolaniguas and Cocaniguas. Both were described by early Spaniards in Ecuador as Indian settlements lying at the boundary between the Yumbos and Niguas. Because of their potential usefulness in helping us to define cultural or ethnic boundaries from centuries ago, we put considerable effort into locating these two settlements. In the case of Bolaniguas, which was in the northern half of the research region, we could only identify a general area where it had once existed. Local inhabitants, most of the oldest of whom have only lived in the area since the 1960s, knew nothing of Bolaniguas and maps were of little help to us, though one river carries the name of Bolaniguas. Farther south, however, the town of Cocaniguas still figured in local folklore, in part because it is associated with the Tsáchila Indians. Some Tsáchilas claim that Cocaniguas was their principal settlement until the mid-1800s, when their ancestors abandoned it due to an epidemic. An effort by a very prominent businessman and politician of Santo Domingo to find Cocaniguas resulted in a lot of local publicity, as already mentioned in Chapter 3. He found a few grinding stones and other artifacts and claimed to have found some tolas (which turned out, when we inspected them, not be artificial mounds) and based his "discovery" of Cocaniguas on such poor evidence. Though he was not conducting any sort of thorough or knowledgeable search, I believe he was in the right area since he used Tsáchila informants. Just as compelling to us is a report from the first mestizo to settle in the area in recent times that he found upon his first entry there around 1960 certain domestic plants that had gone wild. Since no mestizos had lived there before him, we attribute the presence of those cultigens to the indigenous peoples.

At any rate, we have narrowed down the locations of these two settlements but have not been able to identify positively either one so far (see Figure 7.14). The search for these native settlements that survived into the Spanish Colonial Period will continue since the early colonists identified them as important settlements and because they promise to shed much light on the nature of prehispanic adaptations to the montaña.

ANCIENT TRAILS

Salomon (1997) found various references from the Spanish Colonial Period to trails through Yumbo territory that had long been used to maintain close economic ties with highland ethnic groups. I reasoned, given the very rugged terrain and dense forest cover of the montaña, that there were probably only a few principal routes that were used continuously over many centuries, but I had no expectation in the beginning of the project of finding any physical evidence of such trails. After all, how could one find evidence, centuries later, of a footpath?

That pessimism notwithstanding, one of the most fascinating of all the discoveries of this project was that long-used footpaths in very rainy, mountainous areas can in fact leave an indelible mark on the landscape. The discovery was not ours so much as that of some local inhabitants who themselves lived for years or even decades in remote parts of the forest and got around on foot or horseback. They sometimes came across these ancient trails and readily recognized them for what they were.

The physical appearance of these ancient trails is as narrow, deep trenches, especially when they are found on hillsides. The reason is quite obvious to anyone who has spent a fair amount of time traveling through a hilly jungle, as we did. As the movement of pedestrians through the forest in single file beats down a narrow line of vegetation, the ground is exposed directly to the erosive effects of hard rain. The narrow path gradually becomes a slight trough and, as the path remains in use and erosion continues, the trough becomes more and more deeply eroded. It is easy to see these incipient troughs practically anywhere that modern inhabitants beat a trail through the forest, though, as I already said, the effects are more notable in sloping terrain where more erosion occurs. If the same trail remains in use for decades or even longer, the trough becomes a deep and narrow trench. In northwestern Ecuador, the local inhabitants referred to these "sunken trails" that result from erosion as *culuncos*, a word of uncertain origin and meaning. Over time some culuncos must be abandoned because they begin to collapse or they become so deep and dark that it is intimidating and difficult to pass through them. It is not unusual to see two parallel culuncos a few meters apart; one was abandoned and a parallel trail was begun right next to it.

These are not merely erosion channels, though certainly erosion plays a major part in their evolution. Shallow to medium-depth culuncos are found on flat land in some instances and they can sometimes be traced for long distances up and down hills. The deepest culuncos we observed were as much as 6 m (about 19 feet) deep and we were told of even deeper ones. Because these trenches are deep, dark and surrounded by dense vegetation, they proved to be quite difficult to photograph. Nonetheless, I include here two pictures showing Oseas Espín, a good friend and excellent guide in the region, posing at the entrance to one culunco (Figure 7.15) and inside another one (Figure 7.16). That particular trail, by the way, is known from oral history to have been used heavily from the 1800s until about the 1960s. Espín and I walked the entire trail in 1986. Many of the culuncos had collapsed, but we found others, such as those in the photographs, still in passable condition. In the case of this particular trail, the erosion had been accelerated somewhat since it was not simply a footpath but had been used by teams of mules and oxen carrying goods between the montaña and the highlands. After the construction of a gravel road into the region in the 1960s, this trail was mostly abandoned, though it is still used even today by moonshiners who take their bootleg alcohol to the highlands on the old trail in order to avoid the police; we encountered one such bootlegger with a small mule team during our hike.

If I may go off on a tangent for a moment, Oseas Espín, a very modest rural mestizo who had only a fourth grade education, used to spend the long, dreary rainy months at his hut in the rainforest near Nanegal writing down true stories as well as folk tales about that old trail and the region. After many years of occasional writing, he had a manuscript of a couple hundred pages that he tried to get published in Quito

*Figure 7.15 Oseas Espín at
the entrance to a* culunco

as a book. It is a fascinating tale of history and folklore, so I wrote a lengthy fore-word for it and have tried on several occasions to find a publisher in Ecuador, so far without success. Señor Espín died in 1996 of cancer but his family and I still hope that a way will be found to get his remarkable book into print. He was profoundly knowledgeable about the region, had friends and acquaintances practically all over Western Pichincha, and continued traveling around the region even as he was dying from cancer to find answers to questions I had posed to him.

While a few archaeologists who saw pictures of these culuncos were skeptical of our conclusion that these are old trails, we became ever more certain that we were correct simply because we could view the culuncos in various stages of formation as trails and because some of them remain in use right up to the present. We were also able to confirm on many occasions what our various informants had told us: namely, modern day footpaths tend to follow contours around mountains whereas old "Indian" footpaths typically were higher and actually went right along the mountain ridges. Invariably, when more than one culunco could be found in a locality, the one still in use wound around the mountain at a median elevation while an old, very deep, abandoned culunco could be found higher up on top of the ridge. If this pattern is generally correct, then just the location of the paths might tell us whether or not they are prehispanic.

Figure 7.16 Oseas Espín inside a deep culunco *of a trail he and his father used regularly during the early 20th century*

After concluding with considerable confidence for these and other reasons that the culuncos were remnants of trails—some modern, some historic, and others probably quite ancient—I returned to the U.S. and subsequently became aware that similar features had been discovered by archaeologists working in a comparable natural environment in Costa Rica. In that Central American country, the sunken trails were first discovered when they appeared as anomalous linear "tracks" in infrared photographs taken from earth orbit by NASA (Sheets and Sever 1991). The researchers then went into the cloud forest to find out what the tracks were and discovered erosion channels similar to the culuncos in Ecuador. They concluded, unaware of our discoveries in Western Pichincha, that these were definitely ancient footpaths. A NASA researcher subsequently contacted me about making a similar photographic reconnaissance of Western Pichincha, but so far no money has been budgeted by NASA for such work.

How might one try to establish the age of these paths, given that we suspect they range from very recent to very ancient? It might be tempting to look for diagnostic pottery along the trails and to use cross-dating. However, if one stops and considers carefully, one will realize that there is no guarantee that the pottery was necessarily left by someone who was walking along the trail. It is very likely that the trail cuts through any number of archaeological sites and some of the pottery was there before the trail was in use or was deposited by later inhabitants after the trail was abandoned.

Sheets and Sever (1991) approached this temporal problem through stratigraphic analysis. They carefully excavated rectangular trenches across portions of the sunken trails in order to reveal the sediment layers as clearly as possible. These trails are located near Arenal Volcano in Costa Rica, which has a known eruption history that includes ten major phases in the past 4,000 years. Each eruptive phase has deposited a horizontal layer of tephra. By observing which tephra layers had been dissected by the ever-deepening sunken trail and which tephra layers overlay the trail, they were able to bracket the age of the trails.

We have not yet excavated similar cross-section trenches for the Western Pichincha culuncos, though we will eventually test that method. The reason for delay, besides the fact that we have a very long list of additional fieldwork to perform, is that the volcanic history of Western Pichincha is not so detailed. As was emphasized in the previous chapter on the Nambillo site, there have been only three major eruptive phases in much of Pichincha over the past few thousand years, so we could not come up with a time bracket nearly as precise as the one for Costa Rica.

It is likely that the oldest of these culuncos are remnants of trails first forged by the Yumbos, or perhaps even by their montaña predecessors. One culunco that passes through Cachillacta goes very near the deposits that date back to nearly 1500 B.C., though we are not sure the trail itself is that old. Whether the inhabitants that early were the ancestors of the Yumbos or some unrelated nation is a question we cannot yet answer. The Incas, on the other hand, are not known for simple footpaths but rather for a stunning network of wide, carefully constructed roads that crisscrossed their great Andean empire. On that basis one might be tempted to dismiss any of these culuncos as having any relationship to the Inca road system. Such a dismissal could be premature, however, since almost nothing is known of Inca roads in cloud forest environments. Perhaps their "roads" were no different in that rugged and very rainy, heavily forested environment than the trails created by the Yumbos. We did look for physical evidence of the purported "Inca highway" through Western Pichincha, but we have so far found no road that appears to be of Inca construction. The most we could do was find a cobblestone road constructed in the 1850s–1860s as part of a project directed by the president of the country.

This discovery of the culuncos opens up a whole new area of study for researchers working in the humid tropics. I have since spoken with other archaeologists and geographers who have worked in similar environments and have occasionally seen what may be culuncos without knowing their origin or purpose. It was my good fortune that valuable information from local inhabitants and an extended study of such an environment allowed us to make this identification.

The preceding description of earthen mounds, forts, petroglyphs, abandoned named settlements, and ancient trails does not exhaust the kinds of discoveries made so far in Western Pichincha, but it is meant to give the reader a generous sampling of the more evocative finds, all of which require more research in coming years. In order to complete a description of discoveries, it is time to consider the principal artifact categories. These analyses of sites and artifacts are a necessary prerequisite to an interpretive reconstruction of Yumbo culture history, which will follow in Chapter 9.

8/Reading the Artifacts

There were only two major classes of artifacts, stone tools and pottery, recovered during the surveys and excavations, and of those only the pottery holds much promise as a diagnostic category for reconstructing culture history in Western Pichincha. Accordingly, this chapter is divided into a short section on analysis of the lithics (stone artifacts) and a longer section on analysis of the ceramics. The lithics in turn are divided into flaked stone tools (those made by percussion or pressure flaking) and ground stone tools (those made by abrasion).

A STUDY OF A SAMPLE OF OBSIDIAN ARTIFACTS

Obsidian is an amazing substance. It forms when silica-rich magma flowing from a volcano cools very rapidly, so rapidly that ions in the magma do not have time to form a crystalline structure. This was important to ancient stone tool knappers because it allows for very sharp tools when obsidian is used. When a knapper strikes stone such as flint or basalt with a stone or antler hammer, the flake fractures along the edge of the crystals. Because crystals, even very small ones, have a thickness at least of many molecules, the edges of such stone tools are limited in their sharpness. However, since obsidian has no crystals, the flake has an extremely sharp edge, essentially one molecule in thickness. This is far sharper than the best steel blades our modern technology can produce, the downside being that obsidian edges are fragile and must be resharpened frequently by chipping off a fresh edge. Obsidian is relatively rare around the world, only occurring at certain ancient or modern volcanoes. Given its high desirability and its scarcity, it has been a valuable resource for thousands of years. Indigenous Ecuadorians were fortunate in that two large sources of obsidian are found in northern Ecuador. Two kinds of analyses of this material are discussed in this and the following section.

These next few paragraphs are excerpted and paraphrased from the technical report written and illustrated by Fabián Villalba, Western Pichincha Project assistant and former archaeology student at the Polytechnic School of the Coast in Guayaquil, Ecuador. He prepared the report (translated, condensed, and slightly modified by Lippi) as one of his project responsibilities.

The analyzed obsidian artifacts were surface-collected from sites discovered during the 1991 field season from roughly the western half of the research region. Altogether there are 420 pieces; these were found at 24 of the 43 archaeological sites cataloged during that season. In most of those sites having obsidian, pottery sherds make up the great majority of artifacts, though three sites were surveyed in which obsidian artifacts were more plentiful than pottery. The analysis done of these artifacts is based strictly on their technique of production and morphology, not taking into account any possible microscopic striations, edge wear, or sheen from repeated use.

Many of the obsidian pieces were labeled "nondiagnostic," since they lack any characteristics indicating they were purposely struck from a core or because they do not appear to have been useful for any function. These may be debitage (waste flakes) produced during tool manufacture, or they may have been badly fractured after being made. These 116 pieces comprise 27.6% of the total sample.

Of the 304 diagnostic flakes, 162 (53.3%) had been broken before they were found. This is not surprising given that these were surface finds mostly on dirt roads or trails and that they had probably been trampled by livestock or driven over by an occasional vehicle. While it is possible that some of these were purposely broken by the stone knapper in order to produce appropriate size flakes, the lack of retouch along the edges does not strongly support this as an intentional practice.

While most of the diagnostic pieces are simply unretouched flakes or blades (defined as long, narrow flakes), as seen in Figure 8.1, a few of them show obvious evidence of edge retouch or a special function (Figure 8.2).

Of the diagnostic flakes or blades on which the proximal end is present, some conclusions can be drawn about their technique of manufacture. The proximal end is that part of the flake or blade that sustained directly the impact of percussion and typically has some physical hallmarks described in most introductory texts on flake stone technology. No hammer stones or other tools usually associated with lithic production were found during the surveys.

Only one core was recovered during the 1991 season (see Figure 8.2, PQ-18 #1). It is roughly a prismatic core with a striking platform and several longitudinal flake scars. However, many of the flakes and blades (42.9%) contain a piece of the striking platform, and on most of those, the bulb of percussion and bulbar scar, two flaking hallmarks, are quite conspicuous. These signs suggest that most of the flaking was done by simple percussion rather than by pressure or indirect percussion. An analysis was also done of the width versus the length of the obsidian artifacts, but there were no apparent patterns, perhaps in part because so many of the pieces were broken. [This concludes the comments excerpted from Fabián Villalba's much lengthier analysis.]

What this simple analysis seems to imply is that the persons who manufactured these pieces used a relatively simple technique of direct percussion on a prepared platform, thereby producing a variety of shapes and sizes. They made little use of specialized forms or retouch. The obsidian industry was simple, and apparently most of the artifacts were left unmodified and used primarily as knives for cutting relatively soft materials. There were also a number of flakes made of quartz, basalt, and chert found throughout Western Pichincha, but these were almost without exception small, simple flakes of irregular shape and no obvious function. Recognizable and unambiguous tools of such material are practically unknown.

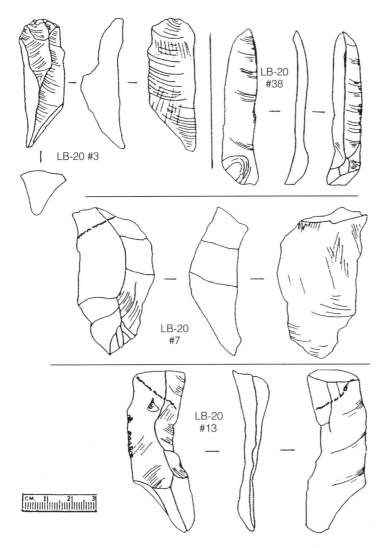

Figure 8.1 Unretouched obsidian flakes and blades from F. Villalba's study

SOURCE IDENTIFICATION OF SOME OBSIDIAN ARTIFACTS

Another analysis was done of some selected obsidian artifacts in order to determine their place of origin. A method of chemical examination called neutron activation analysis of small samples of obsidian can produce a profile of trace elements, and each obsidian source in the world has a distinctive profile. Two of the largest sources of obsidian known anywhere are found in neighboring deposits in the Ecuadorian Andes, almost due east of the city of Quito. These twin deposits are known as the Mullumica and Yanaurco-Quiscatola deposits ("M" and "Y-Q" for short), and ancient quarries have been found along these huge outcroppings (Salazar 1980).

Previous source studies of archaeological obsidian in Ecuador have found the M and Y-Q sources were overwhelmingly favored for this precious resource. Therefore, we had a strong hunch that the obsidian found in Western Pichincha came from either

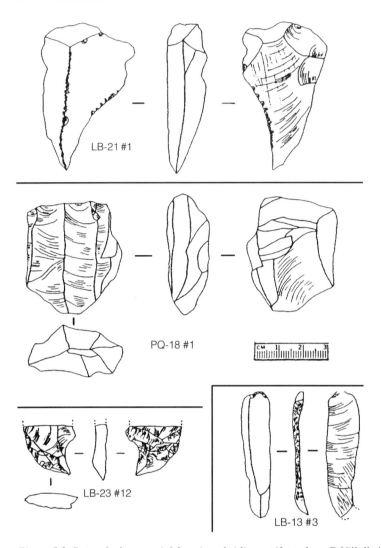

Figure 8.2 Retouched or special function obsidian artifacts from F. Villalba's study

or both of those sources, but a hunch is not the same as having physical evidence. In 1998 I applied to the Missouri University Research Reactor, a nuclear reactor laboratory, to have samples of obsidian from sites throughout the research region analyzed. This is normally an expensive procedure, but the Missouri lab had funding from the National Science Foundation[1] that essentially subsidized most of the cost of an abbreviated form of analysis, and the lab already had trace element profiles from the Ecuadorian sources, which made testing a few of my samples affordable. I selected ten samples from archaeological sites across the region and sent them to the lab, where a small piece of approximately 100 mg was cut off each sample and irra-

[1]NSF grant number SBR-9802366. When the government (as in the case of the NSF) or private foundations contribute money for research, it is necessary and gratifying to acknowledge their support.

diated in order to perform the analysis. Results of the analysis, as had been antici-pated, were that they originated at the twin deposits east of Quito. More precisely, there is a greater than 95% confidence level that eight of them were from Mullumica and two from Yanaurco-Quiscatola. None of them came from the more distant obsid-ian source of Río Hondo in south-central Colombia. These results are illustrated in Figure 8.3, one of a few graphs provided by the nuclear reactor lab showing the clus-tering of the Western Pichincha samples in relation to obsidian from M and Y-Q (Glascock 1999). Figure 8.3 is a computer-generated graph in which sample labels may overlap if their chemical makeup is very similar.

The exact mechanism of trade that resulted in fairly large quantities of obsidian showing up in Western Pichincha cannot be determined, but it is quite intriguing that the western part of the research region, that portion lying at lower elevation and per-haps corresponding to the Niguas rather than the Yumbos, had more obsidian arti-facts than did many sectors of the higher montaña region presumed to be Yumbo territory. This unexpected result will be considered again in the following chapter.

GROUND STONE ARTIFACTS

Most of today's rural inhabitants in Western Pichincha are people of very modest means who try their best to eke out an existence in a region of rugged terrain, dense forests, and nonexistent or very poor roads and are mostly limited to horses or mules for power, not having tractors or other machinery, electricity, or running water. Such hard-working people (and I never ceased to be amazed at how physically strenuous their work is) have always been adept at making the most of what their land offers. On several occasions I met such people who had found ancient ground stone artifacts on their land and made use of them for their own purposes. One elderly man used a stone bowl that was most likely centuries old to store uncooked rice. A woman used an ancient grinding stone in the same way the inhabitants of hundreds of years ago most likely had—to grind dry corn and chili peppers.

Even though the quantity of ground stone artifacts found at the surveyed sites was very low, the sample is augmented somewhat by several pieces discovered by these local inhabitants and shown to us. Most of the artifacts found or observed are known to archaeologists by the Aztec name *metate*. These are relatively flat stone slabs with a worked upper surface that is flat or slightly concave. Food is placed upon the metate and then ground into a meal or flour by use of a much smaller cylindrical or oblong stone, which is usually known by the Spanish name *mano*. Occasionally metates can be fairly massive; we photographed them and left them in place rather than trying to carry them a long distance through the jungle. Figure 8.4 shows a series of grinding stones (metates, manos, and one bowl or mortar) found by an inhabitant in the area near his hut. The slablike metate on the left in the photograph is the common size and shape in the region. Note that the archaeologist's trowel with a 5 in. long blade serves as a scale in the picture.

Four stone ax heads were also found by us or shown to us during the survey. All of them were ground to a flat, ax blade shape with sandstone and then polished to a smooth surface with finer textured sand. In Figure 8.5, the two artifacts with "ears" for hafting are known as T-shaped axes, while the nearly rectangular piece is usually called a celt. All of these tools are believed to have been used primarily for felling trees.

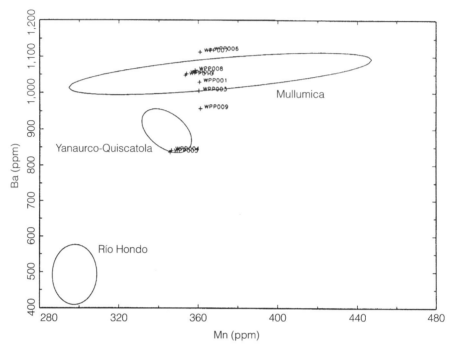

Figure 8.3 Bivariate plot of manganese (Mn) and barium (Ba) for obsidian artifacts from ten Western Pichincha Project (WPP) sites projected against the 95% confidence level ellipses for the three candidate obsidian sources. That is, the three ellipses show the normal range of Mn/Ba for the three different obsidian sources. The pluses labeled "WPP" are the ten samples from Western Pichincha.

AN OVERVIEW OF THE ANALYSIS
OF DIAGNOSTIC POTTERY

By far the most time-consuming part of the analysis of data from the Western Pichincha Project has been of the pottery sherds recovered from most of the sites. A total of 17,882 sherds was recovered during the survey and excavations. Of those, 14,758 came from surface collecting during the surveys, and 3,124 came from excavating at Nambillo. The numbers of sherds that were deemed "diagnostic" (see next paragraph) were 2,007 from the surveying and 226 from Nambillo. That means that about 13.6% of the sherds from surveying were diagnostic, while about 7.2% from the excavations were diagnostic. The reason for the difference in percentages can be explained by the fact that every sherd excavated at Nambillo was collected, whereas surface collections at other sites, if the sample was large, focused on collecting more diagnostic sherds and ignoring many of the nondiagnostic ones.

What is meant when it is said that much of the pottery has little or no diagnostic value? This means that it does not tell the archaeologist much of anything about what culture made the pottery, when it was made, or how it was used. Diagnostic

Figure 8.4 Grinding stone collection of local inhabitant living near the village of Tulipe

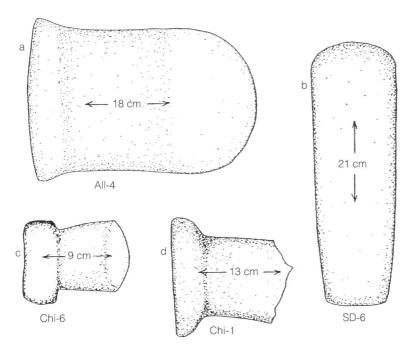

Figure 8.5 Ground stone axes from Western Pichincha

pieces, on the other hand, are those fragments that help to answer any of those questions. For example, if a sherd contains a small portion of the rim of the pottery vessel, then it is possible to reconstruct with a reasonable level of confidence the overall shape of the vessel, or at the very least to have an idea whether the vessel was a plate, bowl, jar, and so forth, and to estimate its overall size. Assuming the orifice of the vessel is horizontal, which is nearly always true, one can easily draw an accurate profile of the rimsherd and, from that, reconstruct at least part of the vessel shape. Likewise, one can estimate the diameter of the orifice closely by matching the rim fragment to a series of concentric circles of known diameter. Some examples of this method are illustrated in Figure 8.6, which shows both the rimsherd and the tentative reconstruction.

Sherds having some decoration are often very useful in ascertaining what particular culture made the vessel or from what time period the vessel probably comes. Other components of a vessel are also considered diagnostic, including the following: the base of a vessel, handles or lugs, spouts, the angled shoulder or neck of a vessel, feet, and so forth. All such pieces are considered diagnostic and were carefully described and analyzed in the laboratory. Although nondiagnostic pottery from the Nambillo excavations could be dated stratigraphically and by association with carbon samples, most of the pottery came from surface finds of unexcavated sites. At such sites, pottery can usually only be dated using the method of cross-dating, and that requires some distinctive decoration or other telltale indicator.[2] Cross-dating of pottery can be done only where the "master" sample comes from a dated context and contains distinctive decoration.

If the truth must be told, there are other diagnostic attributes in sherds besides vessel form and decoration. The type of tempering material used (small-grained material such as sand or crushed rock added to the clay to prevent cracking during firing) or the method of construction of the vessel might be distinctive for a particular culture or time period. It is also possible to do detailed microscopic analysis of the ceramic paste and compare the mineral content to that of various clays from the region to find a match. I have performed all these kinds of analyses in previous projects and hope to perform some of them on Western Pichincha pottery as well. However, they are extremely time-consuming analyses and more often than not do not provide much useful information. Such diagnostic attributes of the pottery have been ignored at this stage of analysis. They are likely to have more value in the future to answer specific questions that may not even have been framed in this initial stage of work.

Archaeological work is very much like detective work. If you have some fairly obvious pieces of evidence to solve the crime with a high degree of certainty, then you do not need to bother with tedious, costly analyses. On the other hand, if your initial study of the evidence leaves a lot of questions, then you need to push on and perform more intricate analyses. Just as in criminology, archaeology requires the researcher to optimize resources (money), time, and effort to get needed information.

---

[2]Thermoluminescence is one method for directly dating ceramics, but it is expensive and may not provide the precision desired. For the most part, pottery cannot be directly dated using radiocarbon or other standard, reliable methods. Radiocarbon dating is out, since pottery does not contain sufficient amounts of carbon, unless it happens to be baked onto the interior in the form of burned food residue.

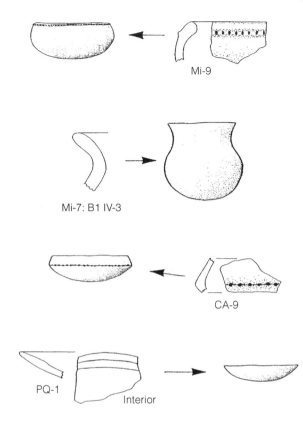

Figure 8.6 Examples of vessel reconstructions based on careful orientation and drawing of rimsherds. Note that the horizontal line at the lip of the sherd indicates the continuation of the rim.

IDENTIFICATION OF KNOWN POTTERY COMPLEXES OR POSSIBLE CULTURAL RELATIONSHIPS

Cotocollao Pottery

Very little of the diagnostic pottery of Western Pichincha was unambiguously related to previously known archaeological complexes. One of these is the Cotocollao complex, which is known from the highlands in and around the city of Quito and dates from about 1600 to 400 B.C. Cotocollao was one of several prehistoric cultures involved in the early spread of agriculture, sedentism,[3] and pottery making across Ecuador. In Eurasia, the development and spread of agriculture and associated technologies such as pottery making is referred to as the Neolithic (New Stone Age), whereas in parts of the Americas and particularly in Ecuador, it is called the Formative Period. The Formative Period on the Ecuadorian coast is quite ancient (going back beyond 4000 B.C.) compared to most of the Americas and has been fairly intensively studied (including several years of work by me prior to the Western Pichincha project). On the other hand, the Cotocollao complex was only discovered in the late 1970s, and intensive research has been limited to only one site on the edge of Quito (Porras 1982; Villalba 1988). We had anticipated that the Cotocollao people

---

[3]Sedentism, the opposite of nomadism, refers to the settling down of human groups into more or less permanent villages.

had conducted trade with nearby western montaña inhabitants or had even colonized parts of the region, and our expectations were met when a very few sites in Western Pichincha produced small quantities of Cotocollao pottery. Whether that pottery was produced locally in the montaña or in the Andean highlands a short distance to the east is one of those higher-level questions that might be answerable in the future through mineralogical analyses.

The vessel shapes, surface finish, and decoration of Cotocollao pottery are all highly distinctive, so when some Cotocollao traits showed up on pottery in the montaña, there could be no question about a connection of some kind (Figure 8.7). I confirmed this by showing the Western Pichincha examples to Ecuadorian archaeologist Marcelo Villalba, the foremost expert on Cotocollao, on various occasions and enlisting his help in confirming my identifications. While the presence of small amounts of this pottery in Western Pichincha was reassuring, there were three additional observations that are noteworthy.

First, the Cotocollao sherds found in the montaña represent only a small part of the total range of Cotocollao ceramics known from the highlands. That is to say, the montaña sample is much smaller and less varied than the highland sample. Villalba (1988) and his assistants worked out a sequence of pottery changes throughout the life span of the Cotocollao complex. While I am not certain that all the details of that sequence are reliable, it generally appears to be valid based on stratigraphic and stylistic grounds, and the pottery found at Nambillo seems to represent more than one part of the sequence. In other words, if one wanted to explain the lack of variability in this pottery at Nambillo as being due to the pottery originating there and later spreading to and developing more in the highlands, that conclusion would apparently be wrong. There seems to be earlier as well as later Cotocollao pottery in the highlands. Secondly, Cotocollao pottery was found at Nambillo in a stratigraphically sealed context (Paleosol 3) and in association with radiocarbon dates that, for the most part, confirm its approximate contemporaneity with the same pottery from the highlands. Finally, Cotocollao pottery was found in a paleosol in a road cut at the site previously identified as Cachillacta (see Chapter 7) and immediately next to the salt springs. On this basis, it could be hypothesized that this vital mineral was known to highland peoples as early as the Formative Period, perhaps by 1600 B.C. or so. Hence, it is likely that trade or movement of peoples between the montaña and the sierra goes back a few thousand years.

Inca Pottery

Although I have previously mentioned evidence of likely Inca sites in the research region, especially the fortress sites, very little Inca pottery was found during the surveys. That is probably mostly because the forts were covered with heavy vegetation and almost no surface collecting could be carried out. However, even in highland forts known from ethnohistoric records to have been Inca sites, Inca pottery only makes up a small percentage of all the pottery present. I illustrate here just one Inca sherd (Figure 8.8), which happens to be the entire rim of a distinctive type of vessel known as an Inca aryballos, a large pointed-bottom storage jar that was normally carried over the back with the aid of a cord through the vessel handles and around the person's forehead, as shown in the 16th-century drawing by a native chronicler in Figure 8.8. This particular sherd was found in a forested area and no other artifacts

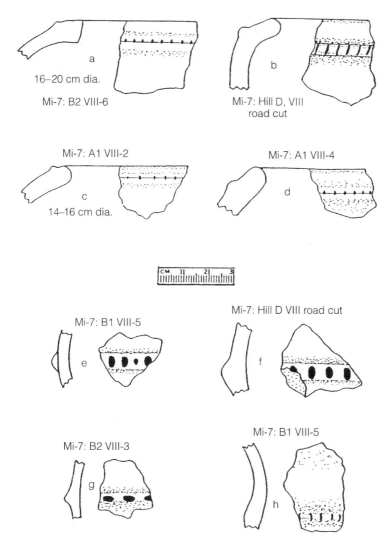

Figure 8.7 Examples of Cotocollao pottery from Western Pichincha

or features were discovered in the vicinity. It is unknown how it got there, although it is only about 4 km from the Inca bath(s) in the village of Tulipe (see Chapter 2). In addition to the forts discovered that were most likely of Inca construction and the historic documents referring to an Inca road through the region, we also have very small quantities of Inca pottery, all of which suggest an Inca presence of some kind in the western montaña.

Panzaleo Pottery

Another special type of pottery that is well known in the highlands as well as farther east in the eastern montaña leading down to the Ecuadorian orient is known either as Panzaleo or Cosanga-Píllaro pottery. There are problems with the term *Panzaleo—*

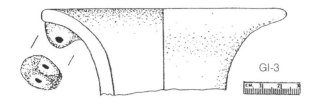

GI-3

OTABA CALLE
PVCLLACOCVAMRA

Figure 8.8 Rim of Inca aryballos and 16th-century drawing showing how these storage vessels were carried (from Guaman Poma 1980: tomo I: 204)

for one, it has nothing to do with the Panzaleo ethnic group identified in Figure 3.1— but we will use that term for the sake of simplicity here. Panzaleo pottery is extremely thin. The vessel wall is typically only 3–4 mm (about 1/8 in.) thick, even though some of the Panzaleo vessels were quite large jars. The ceramic paste is highly distinctive, having a pinkish-orange color after firing and containing ground-up mica as well as sand used as tempering material. The exterior surface is left rough rather than polished, and sherds occasionally display some red painted bands, incised lines, or other decoration, though most are plain. At any rate, this ware is so distinctive that any archaeologist working in northern or central Ecuador can identify it in an instant. These distinctive sherds were also found scattered across parts of Western Pichincha, the first time they had been discovered on the west side of the Andes. Figure 8.9 shows some of the typical rims as well as one pedestal base (labeled "l" in the figure) of this unique pottery complex.

Spanish Majolica

Another distinctive ceramic ware from the surveying is clearly of Spanish origin during the Colonial Period and was not made by the Yumbos or any other native inhab-

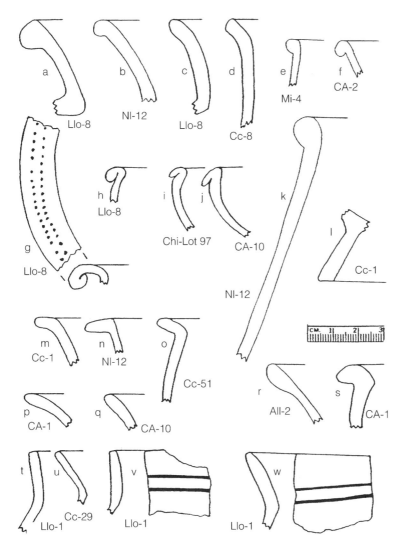

Figure 8.9 Examples of Panzaleo pottery from Western Pichincha

itants. This pottery is known in southern Europe as majolica and cannot be confused with native American pottery. The main distinction between majolica and native wares is the presence of a lead-based glaze on the majolica. Lead glazes were not used anywhere in the Americas (with one quasi-exception in Mesoamerica) before their introduction by the Spanish and Portuguese, so it is a clear marker showing European contact. A total of nearly 200 sherds of majolica were collected during the surveys and excavations in Western Pichincha, and almost every piece belongs to the same type, which is known as Panama Polychrome (though it probably was not made in Panama; see next chapter). The paste is very well fired and bright orange in color, unlike the native pottery, and the surface is covered by a white glaze. A floral or other pattern of lead-based paints that were primarily green, yellow, and black was then painted over the white background. A few examples of this distinctive Spanish pottery are illustrated in Figure 8.10. Again, the presence of this pottery in the survey area is quite significant, as will be discussed in Chapter 9.

Pottery Attributes That Suggest Interregional Cultural Connections

Given the absence of other clearly shared complexes of pottery, the best I can do is to point out dozens of apparent similarities in decoration, surface treatment, or vessel shape between Western Pichincha pottery and that of neighboring regions in Ecuador or southern Colombia. It is now up to me and other researchers to obtain more evidence to shed light on these possible relationships.

There are different cultural processes that, acting singly or together, could result in similar pottery styles in two different regions:

- The inhabitants of those regions may have a common ancestry and, therefore, some shared material culture; one group probably split off from the other at some time in their past.
- They may interact with each other through trade, intermarriage, borrowing of ideas, warfare, political alliance, and so forth, thereby having similar technologies and styles.
- Although it is less likely, the similarities may simply be due to coincidence; however, if there are many quite specific similarities, then independent invention (coincidence) is improbable.

While none of the dozens of similarities I identified in a detailed study is convincing enough for one to be certain in what way different indigenous groups were related or interacted, there are in fact enough similarities that one is led to conclude that there was most likely some sort of interaction among inhabitants of the diverse regions. Just two examples of these possible relationships are illustrated here to give the reader an idea of the nature of the evidence.

A total of five rimsherds (Figure 8.11), four of which have a distinctive cambered rim, decorated with incisions and/or concentric circle stamping were found at two different sites in the parish of Los Bancos but nowhere else in the region. A thorough review of dozens of books and articles on ceramic styles in surrounding regions turned up nothing that seemed identical, though there were at least three described sherd collections from the northern highlands of Ecuador with some similarity. Since Los Bancos parish is located toward the western side of the research region, it is somewhat removed from the possible highland affiliations, and one must explain why the similar sherds, if they are somehow related, do not show up in the intervening Yumbo area. One possibility is that these sherds were part of the obsidian exchange network linking the highlands with the westerly sectors of the research region. The sherds in the highlands seem to come from the late Formative Period or possibly the Middle Period (frequently called the Regional Developmental Period in Ecuador). This has not been confirmed by stratigraphic excavations, but provides a hint of the possible age as well as affiliation of these unusual sherds.

It should be mentioned that while comparing drawings and photographs of sherds from different areas is an important start for the identification of interregional similarities, it really becomes necessary at some point actually to handle the sherds and see them up close. For this reason, archaeologists must be familiar not only with published reports of artifacts that could be related but also with the artifacts themselves.

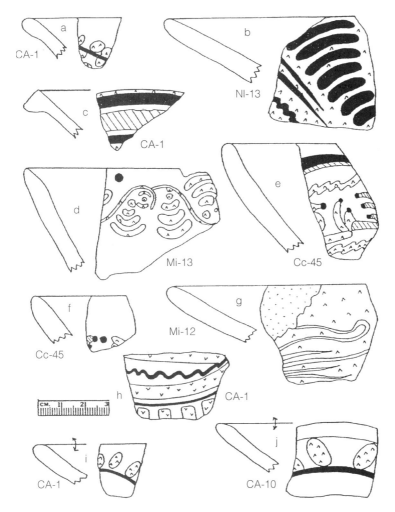

Figure 8.10 Examples of Panama Polychrome majolica from Western Pichincha. On all sherds, the background is white glaze. Yellow is depicted by parallel hachure lines and green by small "v" symbols. The black lines show designs in black paint. The stippled area of "g" indicates that the pottery surface there is gone.

This involves collaboration with many colleagues, with private collectors, and with museums. Archaeologists who have a photographic memory in seeing and handling sherds from throughout the continent and then can recall abundant details of them years later are legendary within the profession. A former mentor of mine in South American archaeology, Donald W. Lathrap, was one such individual.

A second example of distinctive but not readily identifiable pottery is the so-called black-on-white sherds illustrated in Figure 8.12. For each vessel, the exterior surface was covered with a very thin, clay-based white paint, called a slip. When that was dry, a design was painted over the same surface using black paint. While these few small sherds cannot be positively tied to any other ceramic complex, they are reminiscent of a Middle Period culture called La Tolita, known from the

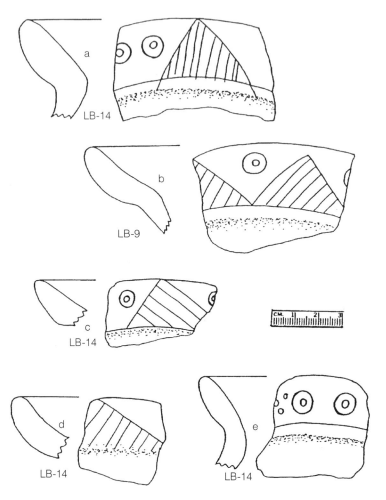

Figure 8.11 Distinctive incised or circle-stamped rimsherds from Los Bancos parish

northernmost coast of Ecuador and across the border in extreme southwestern Colombia (where it is known as Tumaco). Again, we have a possible linkage with another region and some clue as to the possible age of these artifacts. All examples are found in the western (Nigua?) portion of the research region, so it is not surprising that they might be related to a coastal culture.

SPECIAL CERAMIC ARTIFACTS OF DIAGNOSTIC VALUE

In addition to rimsherds and decorated sherds, a number of categories of special ceramic pieces were found throughout the region. Some of these represent special purpose artifacts, while others are merely special structures on pottery. Either way, they are easily comparable to other ceramic complexes and often have great diagnostic value. Again, from several such categories, I pick only a few examples.

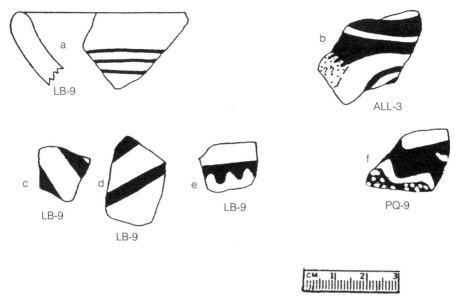

Figure 8.12 Black-on-white sherds possibly related to the La Tolita-Tumaco complex of the Pacific coast

Some flat platelike pottery vessels had small angular chips of stone embedded in the upper surface prior to firing (Figure 8.13). These are most likely food processors and are usually referred to in Ecuador either as graters or scalers. As graters, they probably served a function similar to that of metal graters found in most contemporary kitchens. With such modern devices, you might move a block of cheese back and forth across the surface to grate it. It is generally believed, since such ceramic and stone artifacts are still used in some parts of South America today, that the archaeological objects were used for grating manioc, a staple root crop widely cultivated throughout tropical South America. Alternatively, they may have served to remove the scales from fish, though such "scalers" in Ecuador are often actually made in the shape of fish. These examples are too incomplete to know their shape. If they turn out to be manioc graters, that would be significant information, since it would suggest the adoption of tropical forest horticulture. When grown by tropical forest peoples, manioc often becomes the single most important crop in the diet as well as the source of *chicha,* a very commonly used fermented drink (typically made in corn-growing areas of the Andes from corn, as previously mentioned).

In other projects, I have had the fortune of recovering many human or animal figurines made of fired clay that show more or less artistic expertise. In Western Pichincha, very few such figurines were found, and those that were found are so fragmentary that it is difficult to be certain what they represented. Figure 8.14 shows four such pieces. Fragments "b" and "d" seem to represent the torso of a figure, possibly human, while "a" seems to be part of a head with one eye intact. The only easily identifiable artifact is "c," which is obviously a bird of some sort. Human and animal figurines come in many shapes and sizes on the Ecuadorian coast and from different prehistoric periods; much less is known about figurines in the highlands. Particular

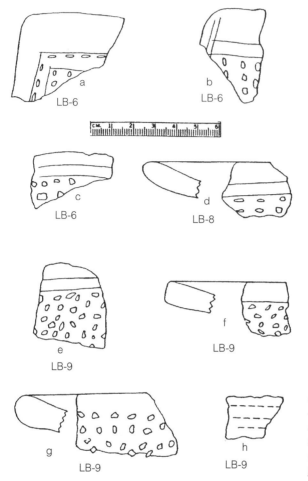

Figure 8.13 Graters or scaler sherds with encrusted stone chips. Item "h" is of the same pottery ware but has incised broken lines in place of the chips.

cultures on the coast tended to make their figurines in a fairly standardized way for a certain period, so it might be possible to identify these more positively when more work is done in surrounding areas and when more complete examples are found in Western Pichincha.

Some of the pottery vessels are bowls supported on legs. Most often nearer the highlands and in the Caranqui area of the highlands, the legs are solid and more or less cylindrical (Figure 8.15, left half). However, farther west in Western Pichincha and then across the coastal plain, vessel legs are frequently hollow and sometimes even given a zoomorphic (animal-shaped) appearance. A few examples are shown on the right half of Figure 8.15; the broken line in each case shows the internal space of these hollow legs. These hollow pieces seem to be related to certain Late Period coastal complexes, but most of those complexes are known primarily through museum pieces lacking good archaeological context, the same problem we have with coastal figurines. Little is known about the precise provenience or age of many of those pieces, a typical problem with museum collections around the world. Unless the artifacts were carefully recorded and removed by an archaeologist, their exact

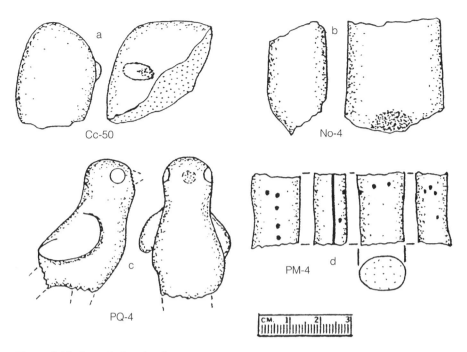

Figure 8.14 Ceramic figurine fragments

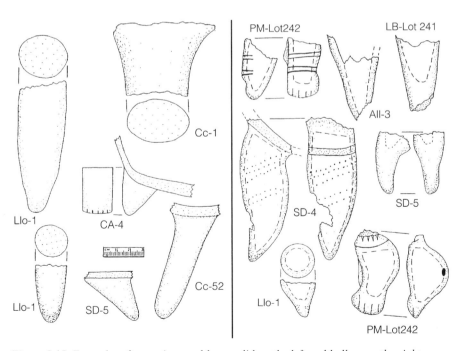

Figure 8.15 Examples of ceramic vessel legs, solid on the left and hollow on the right

provenience and context are unknown, and the artifacts have little or no historical or scientific value.

Spindle whorls are small disklike artifacts, usually ceramic in Ecuador and elsewhere in the Americas, with a small hole through the center. They are known to have been used in the spinning of thread, since similar artifacts are still common throughout the Andes today. In fact, Figure 8.16 shows a woman in Western Pichincha using one to make thread. The whorl fits on the stick or spindle that serves as a thread spool and helps the person keep the spool rotating rapidly; in essence, the spindle whorl acts as a flywheel. The whorls are often roughly conical in shape, though some are more elaborate and may have some decoration on them (Figure 8.17). These artifacts are good evidence for the presence of a textile industry, since it is likely the thread was used to weave cloth for various purposes. They might also be evidence of the raising of certain fibrous plants. The Spanish chroniclers tell us that the Yumbos raised a lot of cotton, and we could infer that spindle whorls are more common in cotton-growing areas, though admittedly there may have been some trade and specialization such that one group grew cotton, another made thread, and still another wove textiles. To complicate things even more, the Yumbos may have used fibers other than cotton, such as wool from llamas or alpacas, or the whorls could be Spanish Period whorls that used sheep's wool. Nonetheless, the most likely inference is that the presence of many spindle whorls at sites indicates the cultivation of cotton and the manufacture of textiles there.

One final example of special ceramic artifacts includes reworked sherds. Native peoples often made use of broken pottery for different purposes. Many native potters in Latin America today use sherds as smoothing and forming tools, and perforated sherds have been used as spindle whorls. As forming tools, sherds might be selected for a concave, convex, or straight surface, and the worked edge is worn quite smooth rather than remaining jagged. Other sherds that are roughly square or worked to a circular shape and having one small hole perforated in the center were very likely spindle whorls. Irregularly shaped sherds are sometimes found with a hole perforated near a jagged edge. In such cases, the sherd was most likely not used as a tool but is evidence of an attempt by the user of the pot to mend it after it cracked. If a pot cracks, people often used a sharp stone to drill two or more holes near each other but on opposite sides of the crack. A fiber of some kind was then passed through the holes so as to suture up the crack before it got any worse. Figure 8.18 shows examples of reworked sherds that probably were used as tools, very possibly by potters or by thread spinners. Another known use of sherds, though not discovered in Western Pichincha, was to grind them up and add them to the clay as tempering material in new pottery.

CONCLUDING REMARKS

While the careful description and analysis of the artifacts has gone on and on in the Western Pichincha Project, I will spare the reader shortly by bringing this chapter to a close. My intention here has been merely to acquaint the reader with a fairly typical strategy that focuses on the establishment of a preliminary database for the region.

The flaked stone artifacts represent a lithic tradition that is minimally developed primarily for the purpose of producing long, narrow blades of obsidian. Most of

Figure 8.16 Woman in a Western Pichincha village spinning thread in her front doorway. The cotton fiber is hanging from the door latch and the spindle is the stick-like spool near her foot. The small whorl (not easily visible here) is just above the thread on the spindle. Her left hand is guiding the fiber as it is twisted and accumulates around the spindle.

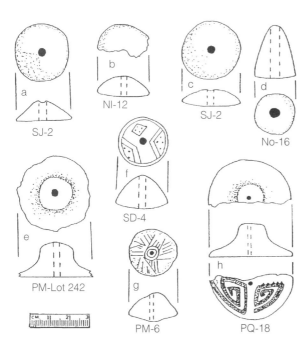

Figure 8.17 Examples of spindle whorls

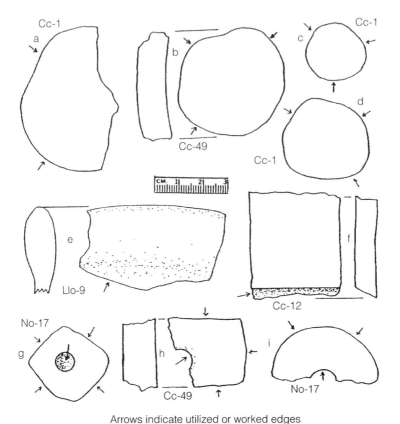

Arrows indicate utilized or worked edges

Figure 8.18 Examples of utilized or reworked sherds. All have edges that were smoothed through use (as indicated by the small arrows). Items "g" and "h" were perforated or partially perforated, possibly in an attempt to mend a cracked vessel. Item "i" is a broken, perforated sherd disc, probably used as a spindle whorl.

those blades have not been extensively retouched and show no evidence of having been heavily utilized. The preponderance of the obsidian artifacts and debitage (waste material from flaking) is found in the western portion of the research region, while obsidian occurs a little less frequently at sites in the cloud forest higher up the Andes. Since the obsidian is known to have originated east of Quito in the *páramo* of the Eastern Cordillera of the Andes, there was most likely regular trade with one or more highland peoples. Why is it that many Yumbo localities—remember that the Yumbos lived between the Niguas and the highland peoples—apparently had less obsidian? Obsidian is so superior in sharpness and ease of flaking to the basaltic materials readily available to the Yumbos in their domain that it is hard to imagine they would have shunned the obsidian that was passing through their territory. This remains something of a mystery. The only interpretation that occurs to me is that many Yumbos might have considered obsidian even more valuable as a commodity of exchange to get other resources than for its own intrinsic value. It seems as if the Niguas had become important middlemen in the obsidian exchange between the coast and highlands. They obtained surpluses of obsidian not only for their own use but also to transport to the coast in exchange for whatever lowland goods were offered. This idea, as ill-conceived as it might be, will be pursued a little further in the following chapter.

Regarding the pottery, a large database has been created, but relatively little can be concluded at this time about some of the culture historical questions that guided much of this research. Some temporal questions have been answered through both the surface collections and the excavations at Nambillo. We know that people living in Western Pichincha maybe as early as 1600 B.C. were making or trading for Cotocollao pottery, and we know that there was enough interaction among various highland, lowland, and montaña peoples in the following centuries that distinctive pottery attributes were showing up over a wide area. It is not, however, until we get into the very late pre-Hispanic and the early Colonial periods that we can positively identify pottery complexes as Inca, Panzaleo, or Spanish. Everything else that preceded those complexes is still not adequately defined in Western Pichincha or in the neighboring highland and lowland regions. Despite this lack of certainty in the analysis, a tentative reconstruction of possible culture areas will be attempted on the basis of this data in the next chapter.

If the survey sample had been more systematic or if a modest number of standardized pottery attributes had appeared over and over again, much more could have been done as part of the artifact analysis. Systematic samples allow the researcher to extrapolate the data from a few representative sites to make statistically valid generalizations for an entire region. The limitations on surveying discussed in Chapter 4 should have made it clear that such would not be the case for this study. A commonly used method of arranging pottery in chronological order by carefully observing stylistic changes is known as seriation, and this method is frequently used for determining the relative age of unexcavated sites throughout a region. However, such analysis depends on the presence of a fairly large sample of homogeneous pottery throughout the region. What we found for Western Pichincha is that the amount of diagnostic pottery is relatively low and the attributes are highly varied from place to place. Once again we were stymied at this stage of research.

Even though many important cultural questions cannot be answered yet with the data in hand, everything that has been presented in these last few chapters represents newly discovered information about the native inhabitants of Western Pichincha. Although there are shortcomings and deficiencies in that information, it is also a tremendous store of vital material. It seems fruitful at this point to turn to some specific issues of time and space as I use the artifacts and site features to begin to define distinct cultural complexes in Western Pichincha.

9/Yumbos, Niguas, and the Space–Time Continuum

Do not let the chapter title make you think the topic has switched from archaeology to Einstein and relativity, though sometimes it may seem to you these ancient peoples have nearly disappeared into a black hole. Now that the data have been presented and several analyses have been done, this is just the right place to try to reconstruct what we know or think we know so far about the native peoples of Western Pichincha. To do this I combine the ethnohistoric information presented in Chapter 3 with the archaeological data reported in subsequent chapters. Given the nature of the data and the original project goals, I have divided this chapter into two main parts. In the first section, we will look at the time dimension and try to create a chronological framework that will guide future research, until that framework is refined or replaced by something better. The second section will then look at the spatial distribution of cultural materials in order to try to identify specific pre-Hispanic peoples and to define in a most tentative way what is known so far about them. Chapter 10, the last chapter of this book, will then follow through on these reconstructions by filling in some gaps with a lot of educated guesses.

CHRONOLOGY: ESTABLISHING THE TIME DIMENSION IN WESTERN PICHINCHA

Chronology may be defined as the process of determining the dates and historical order of past events and of dividing time into convenient periods. Students in an introductory archaeology course will likely learn about the many methods at their disposal for doing this. For Western Pichincha, we currently have data that provide us with five different methods of putting events in historical order or of actually assigning dates to those events. The methods are: stratigraphic, tephrostratigraphic, radiocarbon dating, cross-dating, and historical. Reference has already been made in other places in this book to each of these methods; now is the time to bring them together to construct a chronology for Western Pichincha.

Stratigraphy and Tephrostratigraphic Dating

Stratigraphic analysis is fundamental to nearly all archaeological projects and has been very useful at the Nambillo site and at a few surveyed sites where different strata were revealed in road cuts or in some other manner. However, the presence of tephra deposits over an extensive area between the Andes and the north coast of Ecuador allows us to utilize a special form of this method that is known as tephrostratigraphic analysis. Those distinctive layers of volcanic sediments serve as important markers in the relative dating of sites and artifacts within Western Pichincha. For example, when artifacts are found in a road cut just below a tephra stratum that is known to have resulted from the 1660 eruption of Pichincha volcano, then we know at once that the artifacts are older than 1660 (assuming there is no evidence of mixing or disturbed strata). This is the basis of the tephrostratigraphic method.

Nevertheless, for the method to work, somebody has to do the geological background work of finding the unique mineralogical signature of each tephra stratum in order to trace it to a particular volcano and then, using radiocarbon dating or some other absolute dating method, assign an age to each eruption. In the case of Western Pichincha, some of this work was done by a geologist and a geographer, Minard Hall and Patricia Mothes (1999), and some by an archaeologist named John Isaacson (1987, 1994; he also did some surveying and excavating near Tulipe, as already mentioned).

Three different volcanic episodes were seen clearly at the site of Nambillo (Strata II, V, and VII), and one or more of these have been seen at various other places in Western Pichincha, including the Nueva Era site near Tulipe where Isaacson excavated. In other words, there were three major volcanic periods in Western Pichincha, with other minor volcanic activity interspersed. By comparing the radiocarbon dates from Nambillo, Cotocollao, and Nueva Era with a date that Hall obtained in direct association with tephra from Pululagua volcano just north of Pichincha volcano (see Figure 2.2), it appears that Pululagua erupted a few centuries B.C.[1] Dates from all of those sites point to an eruption around that time, though the imprecision of the dates makes it impossible for now to pin down the eruption any more than to say it appears to have occurred sometime around 400 B.C., give or take a couple of centuries.

This means that anytime a site can be identified as being above or below the Pululagua tephra stratum, we know that it is, respectively, after or before the intense volcanic activity that occurred sometime during the first few centuries B.C. We would expect any Cotocollao pottery found in Western Pichincha, as was true at Nambillo, to be below the Pululagua tephra, since that eruption appears to have put an end to Cotocollao cultural development. Keep in mind from the description of Stratum VII at Nambillo that the tephra was very deep (as much as two meters) and was comprised of various bands of different textures. This means that Pululagua did not erupt just once but at least a few times over a time period that could have spanned anywhere from a few weeks to many decades. When we looked at the banding within the tephra layer VII at Nambillo, sometimes we could distinguish a single eruption. There would be three bands of tephra for each eruption: The lowest one was coarser-grained material, the middle one was medium-grained material, and the highest one

---

[1] Both Isaacson (1994) and this author (Lippi 1998) discuss the possibility that either of two other volcanoes might actually be responsible for this tephra rather than Pululagua; however, Pululagua is by far the most likely candidate, and we will treat it here as a near certainty.

was fine-grained material. Isaacson (personal communication) states this banding by particle size is probably due to the wind currents keeping the smaller particles aloft for a longer time so they tended to settle after the coarser particles.

Because the Pululagua series of eruptions was so substantial—depositing as much as two meters of ash, rock, and sand on the landscape—the impact on the inhabitants of Western Pichincha must have been catastrophic, though less so as one moved farther south and west from Pululagua. It is likely that most or all of the region was abandoned for some time. Whether that period of abandonment lasted several years or a century or more cannot be determined because the radiocarbon records from Nambillo and Nueva Era are not precise enough to tell us exactly when the areas were recolonized. Nonetheless, the pottery traditions that occur in the layers above the Pululagua tephra do not seem to be very similar to those below it, suggesting that the abandonment may have been long enough, or perhaps that the loss of life was great enough, that the later inhabitants were new groups of people unrelated to those earlier Formative Period peoples who made Cotocollao or other Formative pottery. At any rate, what is known for sure is that there was a series of major volcanic eruptions at approximately 400 B.C. and that enormous quantities of sediments blanketed the region, making continued habitation impossible for some undetermined length of time. Therefore, the Pululagua stratum is a very important chronological marker.

The second tephra layer is present at Nambillo (Stratum V) but absent from Isaacson's site of Nueva Era in Tulipe. It represents a less cataclysmic volcanic event; the tephra blanket is thinner and quite uneven over Western Pichincha (and uneven, as well, just within the Nambillo site). Because Isaacson did not find this tephra during his own excavations at Nueva Era, he did not perform a mineralogical analysis of it and is less certain about its point of origin. He speculated to me that it may have been an early eruption of Pichincha, but this eruption must be labeled "unidentified" for now. Nor does Isaacson have dates for the eruption (though another site on the central coast of Ecuador where he worked has tephra that dates to around A.D. 300–500. Judging by the Nambillo radiocarbon dates (Figure 6.8), the eruption resulting in Stratum V may have fallen around 1700 B.P. (calibrated), or about A.D. 250. However, one of the radiocarbon dates for Paleosol 1 appears too early and, for reasons discussed below, I think the eruption may have actually occurred a few centuries later than is suggested by Figure 6.8.

The third and final major eruption at Nambillo can be precisely dated to A.D. 1660, since it took place within the Spanish Colonial Period and was reported in historical accounts of the time. This eruption also blanketed the Tulipe and Mindo areas as well as the rest of Western Pichincha except for the westernmost extreme.[2] Even though the tephra fall was much, much less than that for Stratum VII, it is known from historical documents that this eruption had an enormous impact on human habitation in the region, not so much due to loss of life as to destruction of crops and trails. While aboriginal life in Western Pichincha had continued on after the Spanish conquest, undergoing the changes mentioned in Chapter 3, the volcanic eruption appears to have been more effective in bringing to an end the era of the indigenous people than was the slow-moving Spanish intrusion.

---

[2]It should be noted that a minor eruption of Pichincha occurred in 1999, depositing a thin blanket of volcanic ash over much of the region. It will be interesting to observe how that tephra affects wildlife, agriculture, and human habitation and to what extent it remains a visible stratum in the coming years.

Tephrostratigraphy, combined with radiocarbon dating, provides us with two nearly universal markers, the ca. 400 B.C. eruptions of Pulugua and the A.D. 1660 eruption of Pichincha, as well as a third marker useful only in certain areas, the eruption of an unknown volcano sometime in the first millennium A.D.

Cross-Dating and Radiocarbon Dating

Radiocarbon dates from Nambillo can be supplemented with dozens of other dates from Cotocollao, Nueva Era, and other sites outside the research region on the basis of cross-dating. The reader will recall that cross-dating is the method that assumes the contemporaneity of artifacts that are stylistically and technically very similar to each other. Using the Nambillo chronology as a baseline and pottery as the medium of cross-dating, I searched throughout Western Pichincha for similar pottery to that found at Nambillo in stratigraphic context. Other pottery from the nearly 300 sites was also compared, as described in the previous chapter, to sites or complexes from neighboring regions on the coast or in the highlands. By observing these stylistic relationships, the pool of relevant radiocarbon dates is increased from the original 15 dates from Nambillo to a total of 65 dates for the Formative Period (55 of which are from the Cotocollao site), 17 for the Middle Period, and 13 for the Late Period.

Just to be certain the procedure is clear, allow me to restate it in a different way. Since the Nambillo excavations were carefully done in three very distinct paleosols, each of which was unambiguously separated from earlier or later occupations by volcanic sediments, and since the 15 radiocarbon dates from Nambillo were in correct chronological order when placed in stratigraphic order (other than a couple of exceptions in Paleosol 3), we can be especially confident that the site of Nambillo provides us with a very secure chronology. Therefore, the Nambillo site serves as the "anchor" for the regional chronology. Furthermore, because nearly the entire Western Pichincha region as well as neighboring highland and even coastal regions were affected by the same volcanic events, the hiatuses at Nambillo tend also to be hiatuses elsewhere in Western Pichincha and beyond. In order to increase even more our confidence in the validity of this chronology, I observed similar pottery styles in neighboring regions and checked to see if the radiocarbon dates associated with those styles corresponded with the dates from Nambillo. For the most part, there was a high level of correspondence, as seen in Table 9.1.

Four dates from Nambillo were discarded in this analysis. The two very early dates from Paleosol 3 (GX-12470 and GX-12471) were previously discussed as being earlier than any known Cotocollao dates, even though the pottery associated with them is not particularly early in the Cotocollao sequence. The charcoal that produced these dates may have been naturally caused and may have preceded human occupation of the site. The third date was the lowest and oldest one from Paleosol 2, GX-12468, which seems to predate the Pululagua eruption. Since this date came from a feature that was dug into lower sediments, it might not actually pertain to the Paleosol 2 occupations. Finally, the fourth date that did not seem to fit was the lowest and earliest date of Paleosol 1, GX-12479, which is several centuries earlier than the other Paleosol 1 dates. That date could in fact be correct and simply represent an early occupation in Paleosol 1, whereas the other dates represent later occupations. In that case, it might also suggest that the site of Nambillo was quickly reoccupied after the tephra fall associated with Stratum V. However, there are the 13 radiocarbon

TABLE 9.1   CALIBRATED RADIOCARBON AGES
FOR THREE PERIODS FOR THE SITE
OF NAMBILLO AND CROSS-DATED SITES
IN NEIGHBORING REGIONS*

Period	Nambillo	Elsewhere
Formative	1900–100 B.C.	1870–200 B.C.
Middle	350 B.C.–A.D. 590	370 B.C.–A.D. 670
Late	A.D. 890–1280	A.D. 1020–1640

*Dates are based on one standard deviation (68.2% confidence level)

dates brought into the picture by cross-dating as well as many others for the Late Period in both the highlands and coast that suggest that the volcanic eruption and the reoccupation of these lands by Late Period peoples began around A.D. 700–800. Given this outside evidence, I prefer to reject date GX-12479 and set the eruption and beginning of the Late Period occupations around A.D. 700.

Although it might seem that I am somewhat arbitrarily casting off dates that do not fit my expectations, what I have really done is to come up with three sets of dates, one for each paleosol, that are consistent with each other. I have thrown out the inconsistent dates. Such deletion of suspect dates could be flawed, but it is a reasonable way to proceed, especially when I am explicit about what I have done.

The Historical Method

The use of the historical method in dating Western Pichincha sites overlaps with the others and involves any dates occurring after first Spanish contact in the Andes in 1532. Among these are the eruption of Pichincha in 1660 (as already mentioned) and various other historical events summarized in Chapter 3. Also included is some ethnohistorical information about the Incas, since the earlier Inca expansion into northern Ecuador was part of an oral tradition that was written down by the Spanish in subsequent decades. Allow me to briefly review some of this historical information that is relevant to the chronology I am attempting to construct.

Many scholars have studied Inca chronology over time, and despite the contributions of archaeology, most of the dating relies on the written Spanish record, as distorted as it may be in certain instances. Among those scholars it is generally accepted that the Inca conquest of the northern highlands of Ecuador (and especially of the various Caranqui chiefdoms) began around A.D. 1470 and was concluded about 1490 with the final defeat and subsequent slaughter of the Caranquis at the "Lake of Blood" (as mentioned in Chapter 3). With the capture of the Inca emperor Atahualpa in northern Peru and his subsequent ransom and execution by Francisco Pizarro in 1532, the Inca period was effectively ended and the Spanish Colonial Period began. While infectious disease actually reached South America from the Caribbean Islands or Central America a few years before the invading Spanish army (apparently as early as 1524), any artifacts or ecofacts (such as the horse leg bone at Nambillo) found in western South America probably should be considered no earlier than 1532.

The Spanish Colonial Period can be dated roughly in Western Pichincha using some of the events referred to in the earlier chapter on ethnohistory. For example, the beginning of the evangelization in Western Pichincha by Catholic religious orders began around 1570. It is probably not coincidental that the majolica that is found scattered across Western Pichincha and identified as Panama Polychrome appears around that time. While an Ecuadorian historian (Kennedy Troya 1990:56–57) has determined that no majolica was produced in Ecuador before 1767, an archaeologist who specializes in the study of Spanish majolica throughout the areas of America that were dominated by Spain (Goggin 1968:165) has concluded that Panama Polychrome (which was probably made in Lima, not Panama) was made during the early 1600s. I strongly suspect that the widespread occurrence of Panama Polychrome in Western Pichincha is primarily due to the presence of the Catholic religious orders, since very few Spaniards other than priests and friars actually lived in the western montaña. The fact that almost no other majolica of a later date of manufacture is present in the region is probably because only Panama Polychrome was in common usage until the time of 1660, when the eruption of Pichincha caused an abandonment of the region and of the various missions. In other words, by the time different varieties of majolica became available in Ecuador, Western Pichincha was mostly uninhabited by Spaniards, so those later types do not show up there. At any rate, this particular analysis is based on historical information rather than archaeological dating methods.

Bringing the Chronology Together

Admittedly there is some modest amount of speculation going on in the preceding sections on chronology, but most of it is based soundly on stratigraphic, tephrostratigraphic, radiocarbon, cross-dating, and historical analyses of which we should be confident. When all of this is put together, what results is a chronology for the site of Nambillo that serves as a template or tentative master chronology for much of the rest of Western Pichincha. Figure 9.1 includes the Nambillo chronology alongside previously established chronologies from neighboring regions in Ecuador. The first column is an areawide synthesis of those various regional chronologies. The reader need not be familiar with the other sequences in order to appreciate that there is at least a little resemblance among some of them. This is especially true among the first four regions (columns 2–5), where systematic chronological study has been undertaken and the volcanic history is similar. For column 6 there has also been systematic chronological study, but this area on the far north coast of Ecuador was outside the range of volcanic activity. It is only for columns 7 and 8 that chronological studies have been spotty and incomplete, so those regions are not as useful for comparative purposes.

Future research should help to refine this Nambillo chronology and to add other local chronologies from throughout Western Pichincha. More study in surrounding regions will affirm or modify the tentative areawide sequence. If the resemblance in the various chronologies holds true, then archaeologists must recognize that volcanism has had a profound impact on the evolution of indigenous cultures in northern Ecuador; things may have turned out very differently if only those mountains had not belched so much fire and brimstone! In the meantime, archaeologists working in any of the regions involved have some important timelines for beginning to understand the culture history of their particular region of interest. Just as is true with historians, archaeologists need to have their data in proper time sequence before they can start

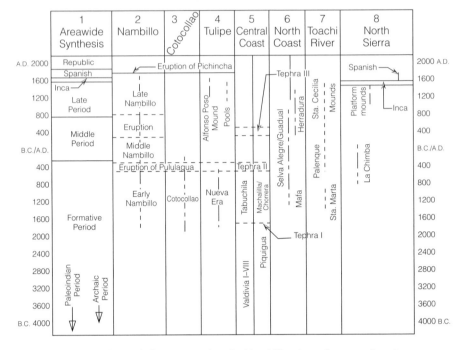

Figure 9.1 Chronological chart comparing the Nambillo chronology to others in neighboring regions

to make sense of it. I believe that Figure 9.1 is an important aid in that process, though much more fieldwork and study will be needed in the future to make it more detailed and precise.

CHOROLOGY: ESTABLISHING THE SPACE DIMENSION IN WESTERN PICHINCHA

If chronology is the study of the time dimension, then chorology[3] deals with the study of regions or, more specifically in anthropology, the analysis of cultural types across space. In the words of eminent Peruvian archaeologist Luis Lumbreras:

> Even though the establishment of a "time column" is of first importance, the establishment of the spatial distribution of types, the task known as chorology, is no less so. . . . Chorology allows one to address the question of "culture areas" that represent the territories upon which an ethnic group had some impact. (Lumbreras 1974:44–45; my translation)

The term *culture area* has been in common use in anthropology for nearly a century to refer to regions of the world in which neighboring cultures shared many similarities due to common environmental conditions, acculturation or diffusion, or possibly because they had a common origin in the distant past. In this sense, the

---

[3]The word *chorology* (or sometimes *chorography*) is seldom used in modern English, but the Spanish equivalent of this word, *corologia*, is frequently used by Spanish-speaking archaeologists, and I find it as useful as they do.

Andes of South America can be thought of as a culture area, and Western Pichincha would be a smaller, more precisely defined culture subarea. I am not sure whether the eastern part of Western Pichincha, an area traditionally identified as Yumbo territory, was in fact home to a single, widespread Yumbo nation, or whether it might have held various smaller Yumbo ethnic groups that were culturally similar but not united politically.

It is always a little perilous to assume that stylistic or technical differences in artifacts or features represent different ethnic groups, cultures, tribes, or whatever. Nonetheless, once one has determined that the objects were roughly contemporaneous (so time is not the variable), the conclusion that we may be dealing with people who are culturally distinct often comes to the forefront. In most instances, the simplest answer is that we are seeing the remains of two distinct ethnic or political groups, though we might also be observing the remains of separate social classes within one society. As with all the analyses here (and nearly all analyses in science), the conclusions drawn ought to be considered tentative and subject to further testing. With that caveat in mind, I will consider the spatial distribution of certain kinds of structures and artifacts in order to propose some possible culture areas within and beyond Western Pichincha.

The Distribution of Tolas

Earthen mounds, or tolas, in Ecuador come in different shapes and sizes, were made in different periods, and presumably served diverse functions, as stated in Chapter 7. For the most part these tola complexes are not well studied around the country. As is true for Western Pichincha, we have some information about what the tolas throughout Ecuador looked like and where they were, but we do not know much more. There are some areas of Ecuador that may very well contain tolas but in which little or no archaeological work has been done, and I am certain that many tolas in Western Pichincha still await discovery because it was not possible to carry out a systematic survey of the vast forested areas. All of this makes the use of mounds in helping to establish culture areas somewhat more complicated. Nonetheless, it is fairly easy and straightforward to draw some tentative boundaries using existing tola distribution data. The hard part is trying to figure out what those boundaries mean.

We could begin by drawing a boundary around the platform mounds (pyramid tolas) that are mapped in Figure 7.3, but very similar platform mounds are found in the northern highlands associated with the Caranqui chiefdoms. Since the two tola complexes are so similar, are apparently contemporary, and seem to be connected by a smattering of poorly reported platform mounds in the intervening zone, it might be equally useful to draw a boundary around all known platform mounds of Ecuador rather than just those in Western Pichincha (Figure 9.2). Uniting this area in terms of a single cultural trait does not tell us what relationship existed among the peoples within this large area. Were they all one nation? Were they separate nations that traded and occasionally intermarried? Did one group invade and conquer the other? We cannot be sure; perhaps the only thing we can conclude with some confidence is that it seems extremely unlikely that they had no interaction at all and that the appearance of platform mounds in both regions is due solely to coincidence.

I have identified four other complexes of mounds within Western Pichincha, but I have been less successful in trying to relate them to mound builders in other

Figure 9.2 *Known area of platform mounds in Western Pichincha and the northern highlands*

regions. Rather than trying to be exhaustive in this study, I am merely selecting examples for presentation, and it seems as if the platform mound complex is sufficient for that purpose.

The Distribution of Pottery Types

Since we have three discrete archaeological periods in Western Pichincha, territories of pottery complexes can be distinguished for each period, even though the chronology lacks detail and the amount of diagnostic pottery that may be related to other regions is quite small. These distributions should be considered first approximations; future research should provide much more detail both time-wise and stylistically.

Formative Period pottery throughout Ecuador and other northern Andean countries is generally quite distinctive. Although there were many different Formative cultures, they seem to have shared certain properties when it came to making early ceramics. Contrary to expectations, most early pottery produced in Ecuador was not crude but quite well made and aesthetically appealing. Technical and artistic skills did tend to improve over time, but even very early vessels were usually well made; sometimes later pottery complexes were cruder. The Formative pottery is often relatively thin-walled (4–6 mm) and well polished, and certain bowl and jar types as well as decorative techniques are repeated over and over. These generalizations come from various regions where pottery has been excavated from definite Formative contexts. I have personally handled and carefully measured and described tens of thousands of Formative potsherds from the Ecuadorian coast. When archaeologists find pottery elsewhere in Ecuador that shares those traits, it is often assumed to be Formative. In the Middle and Late periods, pottery vessels tended to be larger, thicker, and less well polished (with notable exceptions); and the range of vessel types and decorative methods changed.

After a couple of decades of working with various Ecuadorian Formative pottery complexes, I am confident I am often correct when I identify pottery not from dated contexts as either Formative or post-Formative.[4] In some cases, it is clearly similar to known Formative styles, and in others, it simply has that "Formative look and feel" to it. Figure 9.3 shows the location of all known sites in Western Pichincha that yielded pottery that I believe is Formative. The Cotocollao complex has already been discussed, and the area of Western Pichincha that had pottery that is identical to or very similar to Cotocollao pottery is labeled. The location of the Cotocollao site near the north end of Quito is also shown. Many other Cotocollao sites have been found by Marcelo Villalba (personal communications) in the highland area around Quito, but the Western Pichincha sites are the first Cotocollao sites known from outside what appears to be the Cotocollao homeland.

Figure 9.3 also shows an area that contains very small amounts of pottery that appear to be closely related to certain Formative complexes found on the Ecuadorian coast. I previously spent many years researching the coastal Formative and am very familiar with some of those complexes, including Valdivia (the late part of a very long sequence), Machalilla, and Chorrera. It appears that a small amount of trade with those early coastal peoples was going on or, perhaps, that some of the coastal peoples moved eastward toward the foothills of the Andes. In addition, there is a small oval area marked on Figure 9.3. A few sites within this area, including Nueva Era, show possible connections to the coastal Formative as well as to southern Colombia, though those relationships are quite tenuous.

What we can tentatively conclude from Figure 9.3 and the previously discussed chronological data is that the western flank of the Andes in Pichincha province was inhabited by widely dispersed peoples as early as 1600 B.C. The highland Cotocollao peoples apparently pushed westward into the cloud forest to trade and/or settle in that region, while coastal peoples seem to have moved eastward to the foothills. Formative groups living farther north also may have moved into the region or carried on trade there. Other dispersed peoples at this time may have interacted enough to share some of the same ceramic technology. This sparse and widely distributed occupation of Western Pichincha continued until about 400 B.C. or so, when intense volcanic activity killed or made refugees of many of the people and most likely destroyed their crops and settlements.

What relationship any of these peoples may have had to the Yumbos or Niguas is unknown. As will be seen shortly, we are barely able to identify the Yumbos archaeologically just a few centuries before the Spanish conquest; we currently have little or no hope of identifying their precursors two or three millennia earlier. As stated earlier in this chapter, the fact that the pottery found in the Middle Nambillo Period seems quite different from the Cotocollao pottery may imply that the Middle Period inhabitants were completely unrelated to or uninfluenced by the earlier Formative inhabitants.

---

[4]One runs the risk of circular reasoning in this instance, so any conclusions are tentative and subject to future confirmation. In other words, while I have faith in my observational abilities, I need independent confirmation that I am right.

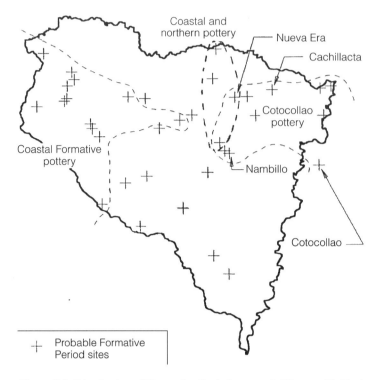

Figure 9.3 Distribution of Formative Period pottery in Western Pichincha

The Middle Period is particularly hard to work with, since it appears to have been a time in the highlands when intense volcanic activity disrupted most cultural development. There is only a smattering of small highland sites known from the first few centuries A.D., and they do not seem to have a lot in common with each other with regard to pottery. At Nambillo, the Middle Period was not distinguishable in some places, while in others it appears to have been a small, short-term occupation that yielded very little in the way of diagnostic material. A little more is known of this period on the coast, but still the archaeological record is extremely incomplete due to a lack of research on the north and central coasts.

Nonetheless, I identified what pottery I could throughout Western Pichincha that seemed to bear some resemblance to Middle Period pottery elsewhere (Figure 9.4). There is only one highly distinctive type among this material, and that is the black-on-white ware found at only four sites in the western portion of the research region. Even in this case, the amount of material and the lack of specific information about a possible source for it leaves me unable to suggest any cultural connections except that its source probably lies somewhere along the coast. The mysterious Middle Period must remain shrouded in darkness for now. Fieldwork in Western Pichincha has only added to the notion that this period in northern Ecuador was one of population decline and frequently of settlement abandonment.

The Late Period, on the other hand, was quite clearly a period of resettlement of the highlands and of rapid population growth. Sites from the Late Period (often called the Integration Period in Ecuador) have been found by the dozens in the northern highlands, though very little systematic research has been done on them. While

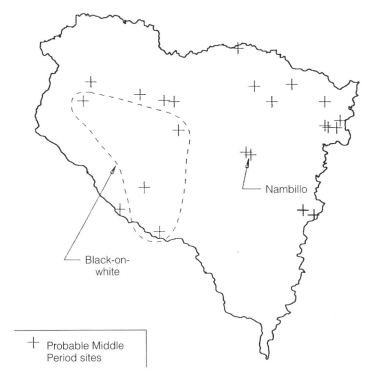

Figure 9.4 Distribution of Middle Period pottery in Western Pichincha

the highland area roughly between Quito and the Chota River to the north is known to have been the territory of the Caranqui chiefdoms during the Late Period, these groups are known much better ethnohistorically than archaeologically. A number of reports give descriptions of a few local variations of Caranqui pottery, but nobody has yet done a systematic study of the Caranqui from an archaeological perspective. We have only bits and pieces of Caranqui material culture but no precise overview of them.

That problem notwithstanding, I have assembled all the sites that have ceramic traits that seem to be Caranqui-like (Figure 9.5). As was done with the platform mounds, the distribution of Caranqui or Caranqui-like pottery could be enlarged to show the Caranqui homeland in the northern sierra. In that case, the map would be very similar to that of Figure 9.2.

Defining Yumbo Territory and the Yumbos

Once we are in the Late Period, we can be confident that we are dealing with the peoples known later to the Spanish as the Yumbos and Niguas. Perhaps the most fundamental question that needs to be answered about these two nations or groupings of nations is in regard to defining their respective territories. Ethnohistoric information presented in Chapter 3 tells us that the Yumbos lived toward the Andes and the Niguas toward the coast and that the frontier was an imaginary line running from Sigchos in the south to the Lita hills to the north. This is a very vague reference, since

Figure 9.5 Distribution of Late Period pottery with Caranqui traits in Western Pichincha

both Sigchos and the Lita hills were regions rather than points, but a middle-of-the-road rendering of this line roughly corresponds to the north-south segment of the 1,000-meter elevation contour shown in Figure 9.6. Another Spanish document identifies the Indian town of Sarapullo as lying just beyond the southern border of the Yumbos; I have identified Sarapullo using old maps and local informants, and its position is also shown in Figure 9.6.

I offer as a hypothesis, therefore, that Yumbo territory is identifiable archaeologically as the region of Western Pichincha where Caranqui-like pottery and/or Caranqui-like platform mounds are present. The justification behind this hypothesis is the simple fact that the region in which Caranqui-like pottery is found corresponds more or less to what we would expect from the ethnohistoric sources about Yumbos, and there is no other evidence to suggest drawing the boundary anywhere else. The region of platform mounds occurs almost entirely within that pottery area. Why the mounds are not found throughout Yumbo territory but only in part of it is unanswerable so far, unless it has to do with the difficulty of discovering the mounds that exist in forested areas. Such is the nature of a hypothesis: It is essentially an educated guess based on logic and whatever pertinent observations are available. Figure 9.6 shows what I tentatively have identified as Yumbo country.

There may be one other piece of the puzzle that will help us solve this question of national boundaries. Salomon (1997:22, 32) found Spanish documents referring to the Indian settlements of Bolaniguas and Cocaniguas as towns lying near the Yumbo-

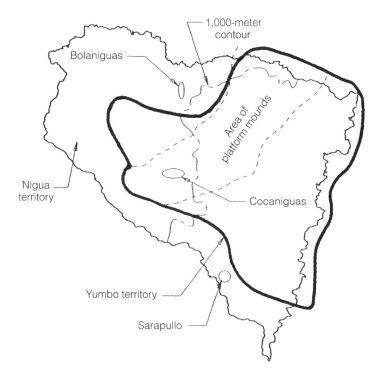

Figure 9.6 A tentative rendering of Yumbo territory during the Late Period

Nigua boundary. As discussed in Chapter 7, I was not able to identify positively either of those settlements, but I have combined information from Spanish documents, modern-day inhabitants, and old maps to estimate their approximate locations (Figure 7.14). These are added to the map shown in Figure 9.6, and they do in fact lie reasonably near the proposed boundary between Yumbos and Niguas. Although Bolaniguas seems too far west and Cocaniguas too far east, remember that boundaries are tenuous and have a tendency to move around over time. All the other named Yumbo towns from colonial documents clearly fall inside the proposed Yumbo area. Only Bolaniguas and Cocaniguas seem to be outliers. This makes me more confident that my hypothesis on the boundary area is approximately correct.

There remains the question of whether the Yumbos were a single nation of people or members of various local ethnic groups who were similar enough that the Spaniards mistakenly considered them all the same. Even though there is ceramic evidence of separate cultures within Western Pichincha during the Formative Period (presumably before there were any Yumbos), we do not have evidence from the Late Period of distinct ceramic complexes within the Yumbo territory that might help us to identify separate ethnic groups.

On the other hand, the platform mounds are associated in the Caranqui region (and for that matter in eastern North America, though there is no known connection) with fairly discrete chiefdoms that controlled small areas; they were culturally very similar but not united politically. The presence of widespread platform mounds over much of the Yumbo territory may suggest many fairly small chiefdoms that could have been somewhat independent of each other, at least in a political sense.

Nonetheless, the existence of a unique pool complex at Tulipe as well as what seems to be the highest density of platform mounds in all of Western Pichincha could be used to argue that a chiefdom at Tulipe was paramount. If such was the case, we still cannot be certain of political unity among the many different Yumbo chiefdoms; we should perhaps think in terms of a religious unity. Was Tulipe an especially sacred place for all Yumbos? Was it considered their common homeland? Was it the seat of a military force that dominated neighboring areas? There is no good evidence to answer these questions, so the possibility remains that one chiefdom may have been more powerful or more central to Yumbo tradition than all the others.

One final note on possible differences among the Yumbos: Salomon (1997) noted that the Spanish Catholic missionaries divided the Yumbos into a northern group and a southern group, with the brothers of La Merced evangelizing the northern Yumbos and the Dominicans the southern Yumbos. He wondered whether this division reflected an old division among the Yumbos or was simply a division of convenience to the Spanish. Though platform mounds have been found more frequently in the northern part of Yumbo territory, they are not really limited to the north, and there is no corresponding ceramic distinction. So far there is really no archaeological basis for dividing the Yumbos by latitude, and I suspect the Spaniards introduced this partitioning as a peaceful compromise between two competing religious orders.

Yumbo-Nigua Interaction and the Niguas

Two other questions closely related to those I have just raised arise now that I have set a tentative boundary for the Yumbos. First, was Nigua territory contiguous with Yumbo territory, or was there, as Salomon (1997:22) hypothesized, an extensive sort of no-man's land of tropical forest peoples between the two nations? And secondly, did the Yumbos and Niguas interact extensively with each other?

Regarding the first question, uninhabited buffer zones are known from other parts of tropical South America, especially upper Amazonia, so this practice is not without precedent. How would one recognize such a buffer zone archaeologically? If there were tight chronological controls on the artifacts and if the buffer zone remained stable over a long time, then it should be visible to archaeologists as a discontinuity in the presence of certain artifacts or structures. However, even where two nations did not get along well and kept a no-man's land between them, it is likely they carried on trade or were somewhat acculturated via other mechanisms; such is common throughout the world.

What I am saying is that it is going to be difficult to identify a buffer zone: We do not have tight chronological controls, any buffer area may have shifted around from time to time, and there still probably was a diffusion of artifacts and features from one region to the other. In the artifactual evidence, the Caranqui-like pottery gradually gives out as one moves westward and the platform mounds disappear, but there is no clear discontinuity that could signal either a definite cultural boundary or an uninhabited buffer zone.

Stop and consider for a moment the United States–Mexican border. There are sharp cultural differences between the two countries and a well-defined political boundary between them, but as one travels overland from, say, southern Arizona into the Mexican state of Sonora, the two cultures, the two languages, and the supposedly two separate peoples grade together. If there were no signs, fences, or border cross-

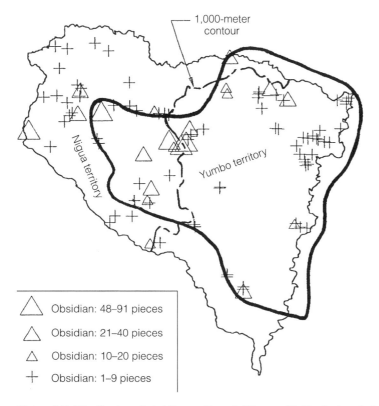

1,000-meter contour

Nigua territory

Yumbo territory

△ Obsidian: 48–91 pieces

△ Obsidian: 21–40 pieces

△ Obsidian: 10–20 pieces

+ Obsidian: 1–9 pieces

Figure 9.7 Distribution of obsidian artifacts in Western Pichincha in relation to the proposed Yumbo-Nigua frontier

ings, travelers might not know for sure exactly when they left the United States and entered Mexico. Imagine how much more difficult the task might be if they had to define today the boundary of several centuries ago (had it existed at that time).

I have one more distribution map that might tell us something about this Yumbo-Nigua boundary or the amount of interaction across the boundary. Figure 9.7 shows the location of obsidian artifacts recovered throughout Western Pichincha as well as approximately how much obsidian was found at each site. On this same map, I have overlaid the supposed Yumbo-Nigua boundary and the 1,000-meter elevation contour, both from Figure 9.6. What can be seen is that obsidian, which has its origin in the highlands east of Quito, is most abundant in the western, lower elevation portion of Yumbo territory but also spills over into the hypothesized Nigua area. There is even a very slight tendency for obsidian to concentrate near the proposed boundary.

The obsidian evidence is of a different kind from the ceramic evidence. I used pottery to help draw the boundary. Each culture in the region easily could have made its own pottery using its own styles, vessel forms, and techniques; such variables are probably fairly good indicators of cultural boundaries. Presumably all peoples in the region made pottery, and because it is fragile and not easily transported, it probably was not an important trade item. Obsidian, on the other hand, is a very valuable exotic good that comes from far to the east. There had to be an exchange network in place for the obsidian to reach Western Pichincha in the first place, and then there must have been more exchange paths within Western Pichincha, as the volcanic glass was dispersed throughout the region and gradually made its way to the coast. Whereas pottery may show a cultural boundary, obsidian shows evidence of trade across that boundary. If trade was ongoing, there may not have been much of a buffer zone separating Yumbos from Niguas.

A possible flaw in this interpretation is that we do not have good chronological control. This obsidian mostly comes from surface collections, and we cannot be sure it pertains specifically to the Late Period populations of Yumbos and Niguas, though in fact the overwhelming majority of surface material was Late Period, judging by the pottery. Obsidian was making its way down to the coast as early as about 2000 B.C., and it was certainly traded frequently over the ensuing three and a half millennia until the time when the Spanish introduced iron tools. So once again we have merely a hypothesis of intensive trade across the boundary; we do not yet have confirmation.

As with the Yumbos, we cannot be sure, on the basis of archaeological evidence, whether the Niguas were a single united nation of people or various chiefdoms or tribes that the Spanish grouped together simply for the sake of convenience or out of ignorance. Since Spanish missionaries in Nigua territory in the 1600s wrote of each major village having its own chief and of the people being known ethnically by the name of their chief (Monroy 1935), our best bet for now is to rely on the ethnohistoric evidence and argue for several more or less independent Nigua groups. Keep in mind, nonetheless, that if there had been unity, it might have disintegrated following the Spanish conquest; what the missionaries observed in the 1600s may not reflect what was the practice a century or two earlier. So far no locality comparable in importance to that of Tulipe has been found for the Niguas. If there was one, it may have been closer to the coast and outside the research region.

There are three other chorological analyses I have performed—one looking at the unusual Panzaleo pottery, another focused on every possible site of Inca influence, and a third looking at the Spanish majolica and the location of Catholic missions. I have also examined linguistic evidence for Yumbos, Niguas, and Incas by studying place names on maps. In view of the fact that the main purpose of this book is to discuss examples of archaeological method rather than to give a comprehensive look at Western Pichincha archaeology, I will spare the reader any more illustrations. What has been omitted from this book can be found (in Spanish) in the original technical publication (Lippi 1998).

10/What We Have Learned, or Who Said Hindsight Is 20-20?

Archaeologists typically spend such an enormous amount of time after fieldwork in the analysis of artifacts that the analyses themselves sometimes seem to be the goal of the research. Naturally, that is not the case, but the analytical portion of the project often takes on a life of its own such that time, money, and even interest may run out before the results of the analyses of sites and artifacts take the researchers back to the people they originally set out to study. I have seen many reports that lost sight of one of the ultimate goals of anthropological archaeology, which is, in a sense, to bring back to life long-extinct cultures.

I have been guilty of this myself at times. The interpretations and reconstructions about long-vanished peoples are never as secure as the analyses of artifacts that precede them. Some archaeologists believe they are being responsible scholars by not taking leaps of faith and not going beyond what the evidence indisputably shows. On the other hand, I believe that wringing a little more information out of the data is entirely justified as long as it remains clear what is reasonable inference and what goes beyond that and into the arena of speculation. Since science is a self-correcting process, it is important to present hypotheses, even if they turn out to be wrong in the wake of future research or reconsideration. One of the great attributes of the scientific method is that our mistakes can be extremely enlightening and often speed up the process of discovery and understanding.

With that advisory statement in mind, let us push the envelope just a little on what seems reasonable about the native inhabitants of Western Pichincha. The conclusions drawn below should be considered as hypotheses that need to be affirmed or rejected on the basis of future research and, perhaps, clearer thinking than I have been able to muster.

A TENTATIVE SKETCH OF YUMBO
AND NIGUA CULTURE HISTORY

Formative Period

The earliest more or less permanent inhabitants of the western flank of the Andes in what is now Pichincha province began to settle the region around 1500 B.C., or perhaps a few centuries earlier. At that time, nearly all of Western Pichincha was most likely covered by rainforest of one kind or another. Some tribes migrated from the hot lowlands of the coast. This eastward expansion does not surprise us very much because it did not involve a markedly new adaptation for those peoples. The reason for this migration may have been the search for new lands or the desire to get away from more densely populated regions. Since the coast was home to early experimentation in agriculture (at least as early as 4000 B.C.), it is very possible that the gradual expansion and intensification of agriculture and increased sedentism over the centuries may have caused overpopulation and other problems (e.g., settlement pollution, soil exhaustion, crop infestations, and conflict among neighboring ethnic groups) on the coast. These and other misfortunes may have motivated the migrations. It is also possible that the wildlife attracted horticultural peoples who also practiced hunting.

Various coastal groups eventually settled in the lower elevations of Western Pichincha, but they mostly, with a few exceptions, did not continue farther eastward and upward into a mountainous and inhospitable habitat. The distribution of small amounts of Formative pottery similar to certain coastal complexes suggests the expansion was typically detained at the foothills. While a little pottery may have ended up at higher elevations to the east as the result of sporadic trade for obsidian and other goods, long-distance ceramic trade on a regular basis is impractical and unnecessary, since any sedentary peoples can learn to make their own pottery.

At about the same time, highland groups in search of subtropical products and salt also began adapting little by little to the jungle, which for them constituted a very uninviting, even hostile environment. This adaptation began with occasional treks into the cloud forest (possibly in search of game animals), and continued for some time until a few small groups learned to survive there and gradually settled down. Some of these groups likely came from the area immediately around Quito and brought with them elements of the Cotocollao culture. The enticement of the salt of Cachillacta, in addition to the availability of subtropical plants, was undoubtedly an important stimulus leading to this early cloud forest colonization.

Adapting to the humid subtropical environment was not the only obstacle for these pioneers from the highlands. They also encountered occasional volcanic activity that had been bothersome in the highlands but was sometimes disastrous on the western flank due to the regrettable tendency of those volcanoes to explode toward the west. Nonetheless, salt, wild game, tropical fruits, cotton, and other products convinced the settlers to remain there for a few centuries.

It is presumed that these colonists, whether from the nearby coast or the highlands (or possibly also from more distant lands), practiced a broad-spectrum subsistence that combined horticulture with hunting, gathering, and fishing. Even though we have not yet managed to obtain direct evidence of these activities, it is very reasonable to infer them, since they were the typical subsistence modes of the Formative Period peoples of Ecuador and since the limited resources of the montaña would have favored them. With the dense forest cover over most of the region, horticulture would have been of the slash-and-burn variety. The settlements, assuming a very low population density and fast-growing forest, were more or less permanent.

The difficulty of clearing gardens in the subtropical and tropical rainforests using stone axes probably served to keep population growth fairly low. In the lowlands, the natives may have settled near the rivers and taken advantage of the narrow flood-plains to plant their crops, among which we would expect to find these typical Ecuadorian lowland and mid-elevation Formative Period crops: corn (*Zea mays*), manioc (*Manihot esculenta*), beans (*Canavalia plagiosperma* and *Phaseolus vulgaris*), cotton (*Gossypium barbadense*), squash (*Cucurbita* spp.), gourds (*Lagenaria* sp. and *Crescentia* sp.), and achira (*Canna edulis*). To this list should be added the careful harvesting if not actual cultivation of various tropical fruit species. Since a wild form of coca (*Erythroxylum novogranatense*) also grows in the region and coca is known to have been an important narcotic as early as the Formative Period, they may also have harvested or begun cultivating this plant. Domestic animals, with the exception of the dog (*Canis familiaris*) and the possible exception of the guinea pig (*Cavia porcellus*), are not known to have been in northern Ecuador this early, so their presence in Western Pichincha seems unlikely.

Some scholars might prefer to believe that the natives of this region were inhabitants of the jungle from very early times, who slowly expanded outward toward the highlands and the coast. While this hypothesis cannot be eliminated, it is greatly weakened by abundant evidence of earlier settlers both on the coast and in the sierra and the complete lack of evidence so far of anyone living in Western Pichincha prior to about 1500 B.C.

Middle Period

This evolution of the Formative cultures of the montaña was truncated after a millennium or so by a series of volcanic eruptions that caused the almost complete abandonment of all of Western Pichincha. Because this was not just one eruption but a whole series, the region remained mostly uninhabited for a few generations. Perhaps within a century or two, some small groups began settling in the newly growing forests to take advantage of the resources. Due to the incipient state of the ecosystem and especially to the poor development of the soils, settlements were few and far between and of shorter duration than had previously been the case. Nevertheless, the volcanic sediments offered a rich mixture of fertilizing minerals that, combined with the quickly accumulating humus, would have created young fertile soils of a very sandy nature.

The recuperation of the natural environment proceeded more rapidly nearer the coastal plain and farther from Pululagua volcano, and the new colonists there managed to establish themselves a little earlier and to maintain strong economic and social ties with some tribes and chiefdoms of the coast. Among their many customs, some groups built small to medium earthen mounds for their burial rites. Settlements by highland peoples were even more tentative, as the cloud forest needed more time to regenerate, but they too found that these newly formed volcanic soils were fertile.

Around A.D. 400 a new period of volcanic activity began. Some peoples were more affected than others, at least until two or three centuries later when the sky over all of Western Pichincha filled with burning clouds. Ash, sand, and rocks fell like bombs on the crops and the small villages. Once again several zones were abandoned, and the cultural development of these rainforest societies was halted.

Niguas

During these centuries, many coastal and highland societies experienced a large, sustained population growth based on intensive agriculture in their respective areas. The unoccupied lands of Western Pichincha and the fruits and other products of the region led to a relatively rapid recolonization, once the offending volcano waned in explosive enthusiasm. Only in the northern sierra, and especially in the Guayllabamba Basin around Quito, was there no such demographic expansion, for that region also suffered the effects of a volcanic catastrophe. Thus, the recolonization of Western Pichincha during this later period probably was primarily from the coast; only later, when populations recovered, did people come from the highlands.

The coastal peoples were carriers of cultural complexes known to archaeologists by the arbitrary names of Jama-Coaque, Milagro-Quevedo, and Atacames. These peoples expanded eastward to the foothills of the Andes and, little by little, due to the ties among the groups and their adaptation to a common environment, came to be more and more homogeneous. A few factors—including population growth, greater control over exchange of natural and fabricated products, and the expansion of certain cults—may have contributed to the evolution of larger tribes and even more powerful chiefdoms in the lowlands of Western Pichincha. Trade in tropical products was increased in exchange for obsidian brought from the highlands. Certain tribes near the foothills specialized in this exchange and in the production of obsidian tools. They also served as intermediaries in the trade between the highlands and the coast. Despite some degree of cultural homogenization, the rugged natural environment impeded any movement toward assimilation, and the tribes remained somewhat distinct and autonomous.

By the beginning of the 16th century, these several nations occupying the lowlands of Western Pichincha, practically from the coast to the Andean foothills, became known collectively to outsiders as Niguas. This was after they had witnessed (or at least had received news about) the fateful arrival of the armies of the Inca Empire and later the arrival of strange, pale-faced, bearded men carrying deadly, thundering weapons and riding strong, swift animals. The groups that made up the Niguas mostly spoke different but closely related languages, they traded goods, and they were somewhat similar to each other in cultural terms. However, it seems that they had no sociopolitical organization to unite them. Each society followed its own leaders, and probably had a territory that included a principal town, a few smaller villages, and a hinterland.

The Incas as well as the Spanish launched their respective conquests from the sierra, and consequently, the Niguas were unaffected for a time, with only occasional trouble but no major disturbances to their lifestyle. Because of their independent spirit and relative isolation from the Spanish domain, they were able to maintain for several decades their reputation as "wild Indians"; that is to say, they were free. While direct Spanish impact was slow to come, the horrible pestilences that accompanied the Spanish to this "new world" did not arrive so slowly. Dreadful epidemics made their way down rivers and along the coast so that Nigua villages began disappearing at an awful rate in the late 1500s and early 1600s. Eventually, the Spanish managed to subdue these groups without battles, wiping out most of their customs and leaving them as if shipwrecked in their own land. Most of the Nigua tribes disappeared in two or three centuries. They were exterminated by epidemics or assimilated by being marginalized and losing their traditional subsistence. Others mixed, biologically and/or culturally, with the new colonists: native peoples seeking refuge, Africans escaping from slavery, and Spaniards in search of gold, land, and souls to "save."

Yumbos

The colonization of the western flank from the highlands apparently began a little later due to volcanism. Despite this slower start, the north Andean societies practiced intensive agriculture. The abundance of their farm production and the general healthiness of their natural environment allowed for a very rapid population surge and a corresponding increase in the complexity of their cultures. After a few centuries of a postvolcanic renaissance, great and powerful chiefdoms emerged in the inter-Andean basins. They competed with each other, sometimes violently, to control the fertile lands, water, and other resources. Between the Andean rivers of Guayllabamba and Chota, there arose at least four powerful chiefdoms—the Caranqui, the Cayambe, the Otavalo, and the Cochasquí—as well as several lesser ones. They spoke the same language or very similar languages and, despite political differences, were very similar societies. Later, facing the fearsome army of the Inca Empire, they were able to settle their political differences and form a confederacy that managed to detain the Inca advance for several years. We have taken the name Caranqui to refer to these several chiefdoms, partly for convenience and partly because we do not know how to distinguish among them archaeologically.

These Caranqui chiefdoms, which were stimulated primarily by population growth, trade in tropical products, and the presence of cultivable land, came to have considerable influence over much of Western Pichincha. I purposely use the vague term *considerable influence* because it is not yet possible to state the nature of their presence in the montaña region with any confidence. We can assume they expanded first toward the west along the Intag River to the north of Pichincha through the sector of Gualimán, where there are still impressive examples of the pyramidal mounds the Caranqui left as monuments. From there they probably migrated southward to the Guayllabamba River and into Western Pichincha. It is also likely that some southern Caranqui, near what later became Quito, moved westward through the various mountain passes of Pichincha.

We do not know to what extent the Caranqui were the principal colonists of the Late Period or to what degree they established relations with other ethnic groups. That is, we do not know if the Yumbos were transplanted Caranquis or settlers from another region that established commerce with the Caranquis and even adopted some of their customs. Continuing linguistic work alluded to briefly at the end of the previous chapter may shed some light on this.

Among the Caranqui customs in Western Pichincha, the most obvious is the construction of earthen pyramid mounds and the less distinctive burial mounds. The building of the structures is not so important *per se;* it is the ideology and the sociopolitical organization behind them that are significant. It is practically an axiom of American archaeology that the construction of large mounds and other monumental structures requires a large workforce, a political authority, and a shared ideology. In other words, the existence of large platform mounds could indicate a relatively dense population with some type of central politico-religious authority. As in the case of the rectangular earthen platform mounds of the Mississippian complex of the United States, researchers through time have presumed that the pyramids of the Caranqui complex of Ecuador had civic, religious, and domestic (for the chief) functions in societies that were organized at the level of chiefdoms.

We ought, however, to take other explanations into account as well. One interesting idea relates to the North American pyramids. Knight (1986) suggests that the Mississippian platform mound is a kind of sacred icon. The mound represents the Earth, which has to be purified periodically by way of its "burial." This burial consists in covering the mound with a new layer of soil. Knight and other scholars whom he cites make reference to the indigenous mythology of the region to support this hypothesis. I present this interpretation, not because it can be applied to the Ecuadorian tolas, but rather to argue that it seems too simplistic to state that the pyramid served as a platform for a temple or chief's house. It is essential that we work toward a more profound cultural understanding of these material phenomena.

The tolas that were built in Western Pichincha, similar to the pyramids of the Caranqui, represent the movement by way of diffusion of an apparently highland ideology to the montaña. Whether this occurred through a massive migration, the expansion of a cult, military conquest, or some other cultural process is not yet known.

The high concentration of platform mounds and other tola complexes around Tulipe may be an indicator of the concentration of both population and politico-religious authority. Just as certain chiefdoms of the Caranqui area grew larger and more important than others, one could speak of the "chiefdom of Tulipe" (our name for it, not necessarily theirs) as the principal one among the various groups of the western montaña. Even so, it cannot yet be determined to what extent this involved a political or religious center. The baths of Tulipe, which are in the vicinity of the dense cluster of mounds, may have had a wholly religious function, but it is also possible they are principally Inca constructions in a location that otherwise was central to the Yumbos.

One must consider that a dense population in the Tulipe zone, presumably based on slash-and-burn horticulture, might very well have caused the deforestation of much of the sector. However, the first European explorers in the region spoke only of jungle, not of cleared territory. Thus, until contradictory evidence comes to light, one may conclude that the environmental changes were not very extensive or serious. In modern parlance, we might describe this as the sustainable development of the tropical forest by the Yumbos. If this is the case, we desperately need to learn how they managed it.

Alternatively, if the Tulipe area had a primarily religious importance for the Yumbos, a very large, dense population would not have been necessary. Tulipe could have been a pilgrimage center with a relatively small resident population and the occasional influx of large numbers of visitors fulfilling religious imperatives. This appears to have been the situation at important ceremonial sites such as La Venta for the Olmecs in Mexico and Pueblo Bonito in Chaco Canyon, New Mexico.

The Yumbos, as the amalgamation of various forest societies of the montaña, had important trading relations with the people in the highlands. The Yumbos came to occupy the western montaña from the high cloud forest down to the piedmont of the

Andes, at approximately 1,000 m above sea level or even beyond. In this zone they were in face-to-face contact with the Niguas, with whom they also traded extensively, especially exchanging obsidian for perishable resources. The penetration of other highland chiefdoms into this territory must have occurred, but the evidence for it is slim. Perhaps a more detailed study of larger ceramic collections and other artifacts associated with such groups throughout the Ecuadorian Andes would remedy this.

It appears that the Yumbos' trade with the highland chiefdoms was more significant and continuous than their trade with the Niguas. The Yumbos and highlanders established (or maintained) trading alliances on the individual, family, and village level. We know for sure that salt, tropical fruits, cotton, manioc, and other produce were taken to the area of Quito and other highland population centers, and we may presume that highland varieties of corn and other temperate and cold-weather produce as well as obsidian were taken to the montaña. It is not known whether professional traders were involved in this commerce, as is known to have been the case within the highland area itself. Nor is it known for sure whether new domestic animals such as llamas and alpacas had been introduced, though I would guess they had been. The guinea pig probably had become an important source of meat by this time, as it was throughout most of the Andes of South America. With the presence of the thin, micaceous Panzaleo pottery in Western Pichincha, especially near the mountain passes, there is more evidence of exchange and perhaps of religious diffusion from the Upper Amazon, if one accepts Bray's (1995) hypothesis that this unusual ware is associated with a ritual feast originating in Amazonia.

Contact

Apparently, the arrival of the Incas in the northern highlands brought with it little change for the Yumbos. Even though the Incas generally were not very interested in tropical zones, the importance of the trade between the Yumbos and the highlanders must have impressed the Inca invaders. The Inca incursion into the western montaña appears to have been restricted mostly to the main trails in order to exercise some control over this trade. Other than trade route control, there is no evidence of forced migrations or of political control in the area. Because of the very short duration of Inca dominion in northern Ecuador (only about 40 years), the Yumbos managed to survive this invasion as much through their relative geographic isolation as due to the importance of their trade. One piece of evidence supporting this is the fact that they did not give up their traditional languages in exchange for Quichua, the Inca language, which was forcibly imposed upon the vanquished in other parts of the empire.

One cannot draw the same conclusion with respect to the Spanish. Although those Europeans delayed several decades in making their presence felt directly in Yumbo country, the horrible infectious diseases, especially smallpox and measles, that came to the Americas with the Spanish began taking a very heavy toll on the Yumbos almost immediately. Their numbers plummeted, primarily through virulent epidemics. Within 20 years, the Yumbo population was reduced to half, and through the following century the Yumbos all but disappeared. Immediately after the Spanish conquest in 1532, the Yumbos were also affected by unknown numbers of Inca refugees hiding out in Western Pichincha. This may have contributed to the reputation that developed of the montaña Indians as very fierce and rebellious, which led to increased Spanish repression of those groups.

Those that survived death from unknown disease and military reprisals had to face the gradually growing impact of Spanish evangelization and colonization, especially from the 1570s until 1660, when Pichincha volcano erupted and made life in Western Pichincha extremely difficult for everyone. Due to epidemics, the volcanic eruption, and forced work at small textile mills, on roads, in mines, and on large farms, the catastrophic decline of the Yumbo population continued unabated. The efforts of the Catholic missionaries attacked the very core of traditional ideology, resulting in the gradual acculturation of the Yumbos. Vestiges of this indoctrination period can be seen in the glazed majolica, which belonged to Spaniards of the first half of the 17th century.

In 1660 the eruption of the Pichincha volcano buried the lands of Indians, Spaniards, and mestizos alike. This geologic event certainly caused alarm, hunger, and a forced migration, contributing even more to the assimilation of the Yumbos. With the new trails opened following the Spanish conquest that favored highland trade with the southern coast of Ecuador, especially Guayaquil, rather than the northern coast, the traditional system of exchange also failed. One catastrophe was heaped upon another. The ultimate fate of these societies is considered in the final section.

METHODOLOGICAL CONTRIBUTIONS OF THE PROJECT

It is hoped that most archaeological projects will make at least two kinds of contributions. The first, which has been the emphasis of these last two chapters, is increased knowledge about specific past cultures such as the Yumbos and Niguas. The second involves innovation in terms of theory and methodology—that is, the processes of recovering data and analyzing and interpreting it ought to be improved in some modest way. While there has certainly been no theoretical breakthrough of any kind in this project, I submit that it has provided some small methodological innovations that may prove to be useful to archaeologists working elsewhere.

First and foremost is the successful completion of a large-scale archaeological survey in a region of rugged land covered by tropical forests of the type that most archaeologists previously considered "unsurveyable." For the past few decades, a major topic discussed by archaeologists has been the need to adopt truly "scientific" strategies for archaeological surveying using systematic sampling and quantitative analysis. Despite the best intentions of many outstanding scholars/surveyors, their criteria and procedures simply are not feasible in many regions of the world, including Western Pichincha.

We did not go into the project with any brilliant ideas about how to solve this dilemma but simply plunged in using trial-and-error methods. As the adage goes: "Fools rush in where wise men fear to tread." Our methods, described in Chapter 4 and alluded to elsewhere, were improvised, and taken together, they constitute a surveying strategy that is anything but systematic; I prefer to label it "opportunistic." It has less value than a truly systematic survey, but it obviously has far more value than no survey at all. While the individual techniques and methods will vary from place to place, the overall strategy of opportunistic surveying is easily transferable to many other particularly challenging regions of the world. I am certainly not the first person to use such improvisation—archaeologists in general are great improvisers in the face of adversity—but perhaps too much emphasis has been given in recent decades to doing surveys "by the book," and I hope this study helps to overcome that bias.

I have occasionally in this book alluded to funding limitations and commented on how we were or were not able to conduct certain expensive analyses. Despite the generosity of the sponsors of this project (institutions gratefully mentioned in the Acknowledgments section of the Preface to this book), the entire project was run on a shoestring budget with very minimal financing. The crew was always very small, lack of adequate transportation was a continual problem, and salaries were negligible. Nonetheless, even such a small operation working under difficult circumstances can, when given enough time, accomplish quite a bit. Perhaps there is a lesson to be learned from that. In fact, throughout much of the history of archaeology, independently wealthy archaeologists and archaeologists backed by wealthy patrons (individuals or institutions) have monopolized research and attention in some areas of the world. Much more modest projects, however, can contribute much valuable knowledge and keep the discipline somewhat "democratic," as I hope this book has shown.

While the excavations conducted at Nambillo were very restricted in extent and purpose, they did reveal that the acidic tropical soils and volcanic explosions did not completely erase the archaeological record. Though subsistence and environmental data may be very difficult to obtain, some evidence of the settlements and associated activities is intact. Other archaeologists working in tropical forest areas have found better or worse conditions, but at least we can now be confident that more extensive excavations at Nambillo and elsewhere in the region will be very worthwhile.

I would also suggest that the use of systematic soil coring and phosphate testing at Nambillo were quite successful in revealing both the ancient landforms at the site and the archaeological "hot spots." These methods, when used together, have much to offer archaeologists working at fairly deeply buried sites, at sites with dense forest cover, and at multicomponent sites with relatively thick and discrete strata.

Finally, though not really a methodological contribution, mention should be made again of the most unexpected and intriguing discovery of ancient footpaths (the culuncos) in the mountainous rainforest. I have now presented photographs and data on the eroded paths at a few archaeological conferences, and many of my colleagues have begun to take note. Some have even mentioned that they observed similar features without any idea of what they might be. I am convinced that these are in fact ancient trails, and sharing this discovery with other archaeologists working in similar environments worldwide can only have a positive and stimulating effect on archaeological work far beyond Western Pichincha.

But ancient peoples, not modern methods, are the focus of this study, so I will conclude with some comments about the fate of those people, keeping in mind that this project is far from over and that what has been learned so far is only the beginning.

THE LOST RAINFOREST:
THE FATE OF THE NIGUAS AND YUMBOS

In Chapter 2, I lamented to a certain extent the chaotic contemporary development of Western Pichincha, but at the same time I had to admit some ambiguity toward that process, which has allowed this archaeological project to take place. From the very beginning of the project, I have felt a profound enchantment toward the region and a desire to see it protected against massive, unplanned human development.

I also mentioned in that chapter the fact that the region has remained mostly forgotten in Ecuador, since historically it has not entered into the national consciousness to any great extent. Until very recently, the western montaña of Pichincha was nearly invisible. The contradiction is obvious: It was just that invisibility that saved the western montaña until modern times, and it is the recent invasion by thousands of modern-day colonists and, even more recently, tourists that is destroying it.

I have not tried to portray Western Pichincha as some sort of paradise, nor the Yumbos and Niguas as "noble savages." Most of the world has been altered by humans, and thousands of human societies have become extinct. One could interpret prehistory and history as the gradual destruction of the earth and of human diversity, and there is at least a kernel of truth in such a synthesis. On the other hand, one could interpret ethnocide (the destruction of cultures) as a component of ethnogenesis (the birth of new cultures): With the assimilation of one culture, a hybrid culture may be born with new adaptations and new potential.

The problem (and not just in Ecuador but around the world) is that it is very difficult to find traces of these indigenous cultures in contemporary societies. We do not know that much yet about the Yumbos and Niguas, but who would dare to state that the contemporary colonization of Western Pichincha is guided by the values and knowledge of its native inhabitants? Personally, I consider the disappearance of such long-lived societies a tragedy, even though the process is so common in the world. Perhaps the greater tragedy for humanity is the loss of their knowledge, their wisdom, and their adaptations that permitted them to survive for thousands of years in the tropical rainforests. Modern humans only know how to "conquer" this environment, not how to survive in it, and this conquest is tantamount to destruction.

Among the native surviving groups on the coast and in the greater western montaña of Ecuador, there are the Chachis in the coastal province of Esmeraldas. Their origin may very well have been in the northern highlands, but for at least the last several centuries, they have been "Niguas." Also, in the western montaña of extreme northern Ecuador and southern Colombia, there are tiny enclaves of the native group of Awa-Kwaiker, refugees from the north Ecuadorian coast who may still conserve something of Nigua culture, though that is far from certain. It has not been fully studied to what degree the mestizo and black rural folks of the north coast retain any cultural traces of the Niguas, but it is obviously very little if any at all.

Finally, on eight very small reserves near the city of Santo Domingo of the Colorados and just south of the research region, there are the Tsáchilas, whom you first met in Chapter 1. Their exact relationship to the Niguas and Yumbos is still uncertain, but their presence in the southern part of Western Pichincha, in Yumbo territory, during the last few centuries is verified. This ethnic minority of some 1,000 persons, which is currently battling against cultural erosion and loss of land, most likely constitutes the last surviving enclave of what was once some 25,000 native inhabitants of Yumbo country.

The Yumbos disappeared in the midst of high mortality, emigration, and acculturation. With their disappearance they were not simply forgotten; their fate has been even more humiliating than that. In Ecuador the disappearance of the true Yumbos allowed for the use of their name to refer incorrectly to the Quichua-speaking Indian inhabitants of the eastern slope of the Andes above Amazonia, so that even Ecuadorians today are confused about who the Yumbos used to be. In a poignant display of tragic irony, the marketing department of a corporation in Spain has taken

"Yumbo" as the brand name for their toilet paper. With the possible exception of the Tsáchilas and perhaps an occasional cultural remnant among highland or coastal Indians, there are no more Yumbos. Their name was taken over and their lands were abandoned until the second half of the 20th century and early 21st century, when the recent and accelerating colonization of Western Pichincha threatens the destruction not only of their natural habitat but even of the last archaeological vestiges of their culture.

References

Bray, Tamara. 1995. The Panzaleo puzzle: Non-local pottery in northern highland Ecuador. *Journal of Field Archaeology* 22(2): 137–156.

Cabello Balboa, Miguel. 1945 [originally published 1579?]. Verdadera Descripción y Relación Larga de la Provincia y Tierra de las Esmeraldas. *Obras de Miguel Cabello Balboa*, vol. 1, editado por Jacinto Jijón y Caamaño, Editorial Ecuatoriana, Quito.

Cabello Balboa, Miguel. 1951 [originally published 1586]. *Miscelánea Antártica*, Instituto de Etnología, Seminario de Historia del Perú-Incas. Universidad Nacional Mayor de San Marcos, Lima.

Cieza de León, Pedro. 1962 [originally published 1553]. *La Crónica del Perú* (Primera Parte). Espasa-Calpe, Madrid.

DeBoer, Warren R. 1995. Returning to Pueblo Viejo: History and archaeology of the Chachi (Ecuador). In *Archaeology in the Lowland American Tropics: Current Analytical Methods and Applications*, edited by Peter W. Stahl, pp. 243–262, Cambridge University Press, Cambridge.

Eidt, Robert C. 1984. *Advances in Abandoned Settlement Analysis: Applications to Prehistoric Anthrosols in Colombia, South America*. The Center for Latin America, University of Wisconsin, Milwaukee.

Glascock, Michael D. 1999. Sources of obsidian artifacts from Pichincha province, Ecuador. Unpublished technical report, Missouri University Research Reactor, Columbia, Missouri.

Goggin, John M. 1968. *Spanish Majolica in the New World: Types of the Sixteenth to Eighteenth Centuries*. Yale University Publications in Anthropology No. 72, Yale University, New Haven, Connecticut.

Gondard, Pierre, and Freddy López. 1983. *Inventario Arqueológico Preliminar de los Andes Septentrionales del Ecuador*. Ministerio de Agricultura y Ganadería, Quito.

Guaman Poma de Ayala, Felipe. 1980 [written 1612–1616]. *El Primer Nueva Corónica y Buen Gobierno, Tomo I*. Siglo Vientiuno Editores, México, D.F.

Hall, Minard L., and Patricia A. Mothes. 1999. La actividad volcánica del Holoceno en el Ecuador y Colombia austral: Impedimento al desarrollo de las civilizaciones pasadas. En *Actividad Volcánica y Pueblos Precolombinos en el Ecuador*, editado por Patricia A. Mothes, pp. 11–40, Ediciones Abya-Yala, Quito.

Isaacson, John. 1982. Proyecto Tulipe. Investigaciones arqueológicas en el noroccidente del Pichincha. Paper presented at Coloquio Internacional "Carlos Zevallos Menéndez", Guayaquil, Ecuador.

Isaacson, John. 1987. Volcanic activity and human occupation of the northern Andes: The application of tephrostratigraphic techniques to the problem of human settlement in the western montaña. Ph.D. dissertation, University of Illinois, Champaign-Urbana.

Isaacson, John. 1994. Volcanic sediments in archaeological contexts from western Ecuador. In *Regional Archaeology in Northern Manabí, Ecuador, Volume 1: Environment, Cultural Chronology, and Prehistoric Subsistence in the Jama River Valley*, edited by James A. Zeidler and Deborah M. Pearsall, pp. 131–140, University of Pittsburgh and Ediciones Libri Mundi, Pittsburgh, Pennsylvania.

Jara, Holguer. n.d. Excavaciones arqueológicas y restauración de las piscinas de Tulipe. Unpublished manuscript, Museos del Banco Central del Ecuador, Quito.

Kennedy Troya, Alexandra. 1990. Apuntes sobre arquitectura en barro y cerámica en la colonia. En *Cerámica Colonial y Vida Cotidiana*, coordinado por Jaime Idrovo y Alexandra Kennedy Troya, pp. 39–59, Fundación Paul Rivet, Cuenca, Ecuador.

Knight, James Vernon, Jr. 1986. The institutional organization of Mississippian religion. *American Antiquity 51*(4): 675–687.

Limbrey, Susan. 1975. *Soil Science and Archaeology*. Academic Press, New York.

Lippi, Ronald D. 1988. Paleotopography and phosphate analysis of a buried jungle site in Ecuador. *Journal of Field Archaeology* 15(1): 85–97.

Lippi, Ronald D. 1996. *La Primera Revolución Ecuatoriana: El Desarrollo de la Vida Agrícola en el Antiguo Ecuador*. Marka: Instituto de Historia y Antropología Andinas, Quito.

Lippi, Ronald D. 1998. *Una Exploración Arqueológica del Pichincha Occidental, Ecuador*. Museo Jacinto Jijón y Caamaño de la Pontificia Universidad Católica del Ecuador, Consejo Provincial de Pichincha, y Banco Interamericano de Desarrollo, Quito.

Lippi, Ronald D. 2001. Yumbo demographics before and after 1532. Paper presented at the 29th Midwest Conference of Andean and Amazonian Archaeology and Ethnohistory, University of Michigan, Ann Arbor.

Lubensky, Earl. 1988. Prospección arqueológica, Hacienda La Florida, Santo Domingo de los Colorados, enero 1979. Paper presented at the symposium, "1977–1987: Ten Years of Ecuadorian Archaeology," Cuenca, Ecuador.

Lumbreras, Luis. 1974. *La Arqueología Como Ciencia Social*. Ediciones Librerías Allende, S.A., México, D.F.

Monroy, Joel L. 1935. *Los Religiosos de La Merced en la Costa del Antiguo Reino de Quito*. Editorial Labor, Quito.

Palop Martínez, Josefina. 1986. Los Cayapas en el Siglo XVI. En *Arqueología y Etnohistoria del Sur de Colombia y Norte del Ecuador*, Miscelánea Antropológica Ecuatoriana, Serie Monográfica 6, editada por José Alcina Franch y Segundo Moreno

Yánez, pp. 231–252, Museos del Banco Central del Ecuador y Abya-Yala, Quito.

Porras, Pedro I. 1982. *Arqueología de Quito: I Fase Cotocollao*. Centro de Investigaciones Arqueológicas, Pontificia Universidad Católica del Ecuador, Quito.

Ramsey, Christopher Bronk. 1995. OxCal (vers. 2.18) ^{14}C calibration software. Oxford Radiocarbon Accelerator Unit, Oxford University, Oxford.

Salazar, Ernesto. 1980. *Talleres Prehistóricos en los Altos Andes del Ecuador*. Universidad de Cuenca, Cuenca, Ecuador.

Salomon, Frank. 1997. *Los Yumbos, Niguas y Tsáchila o "Colorados" Durante la Colonia Española: Etnohistoria del Noroccidente de Pichincha, Ecuador*. Ediciones Abya-Yala, Quito.

Salomon, Frank, and Clark Erickson. 1984. Tulipe, un recinto sagrado en la montaña ecuatoriana. *Antropología Ecuatoriana 2*: 57–78, Quito.

Sheets, Payson, and Thomas L. Sever. 1991. Prehistoric footpaths in Costa Rica: Transportation and communication in a tropical rainforest. In *Ancient Road Networks and Settlement Hierarchies in the New World*, edited by Charles D. Trombold, pp. 53–64, Cambridge University Press, Cambridge.

Stein, Julie K. 1986. Coring archaeological sites. *American Antiquity 51*(3): 505–527.

Stuiver, M., and R. S. Kra (eds.). 1986. Calibration, Proceedings of the 12th International [14]C Conference. *Radiocarbon 28*(2): 805–1030.

Velástegui, Holguer. 1989. *Los Colorados*. Editora Luz de América, Quito Villalba, Marcelo.

Villalba, Marcelo. 1988. *Cotocollao: Una Aldea Formativa del Valle de Quito*. Miscelánea Antropológica Ecuatoriana, Serie Monográfica 2. Museos del Banco Central del Ecuador, Quito.

Credits

Figure 1.2   Photo by Chuck Lippi, ca. 1969
Figure 5.2   Map simplified by author from detailed topographic map created by
              Segundo Enríquez, 1985
Figure 5.3   Photo of author by Marco Suárez, project assistant
Figure 6.8   Radiocarbon calibrations performed and graph created using OxCal
              software by Ramsey (1995), Oxford University
Figure 8.1   Drawing by Fabián Villalba, project assistant
Figure 8.2   Drawing by Fabián Villalba, project assistant
Figure 8.3   Plot by Glascock (1999), Missouri University Research Reactor
Figure 8.8   Drawing below rimsherd is from Guaman Poma 1980: tomo I: 204
              and is originally from Guaman Poma's early 17th-century manuscript,
              now in the public domain

All other photographs, illustrations, and tables were prepared by the author, including most of the maps, which he created using Cadkey drafting software.

Index